SiMPlY Write!

Practical
Advice
for Personal
and
Family
Writing

VERA GOODMAN

EDITORS

Rod Chapman / Elizabeth Collins Oman

Reading Wings™

Copyright © 2005 by Vera Goodman

1st printing 2005

Publisher: **Reading Wings Inc.**, Calgary, Alberta, Canada
                 1-800-411-9660

ISBN 0-9699938-3-8

Canadian Cataloguing in Publication Data

Goodman, Vera Elizabeth, 1934-
  Simply write: practical advice for personal and family writing
  /Vera Goodman.

  Includes bibliographical references.
  ISBN 0-9699938-3-8

  1. Language acquisition – Parent participation. II. English language – Composition and exercises – Study and teaching (Preschool)   III. English language – Composition and exercises – Study and teaching (Elementary) IV. Authorship   I. Title.

LB1576.G67 2005   372.13'028'1   C2005-905353-1

Design:
Gail Pocock, Bulldog Communications Inc.
Calgary, Alberta, Canada (403) 228-9861

Photography:
PHOTOGRAPHY – Trudie Lee Photography

Printing:
Friesen Printers
Ste. 120, 3016 - 19th St. N.E., Calgary, Alberta, Canada T2E 6Y9

Printed and Bound in Canada

This book is dedicated to my grandchildren
Sean, Bryce and Rachel
whose songs and stories keep me
young at heart.

And to my mother, Thelma Lockhart,
a remarkable woman
who is an exemplary model
to her family.

Table of Contents

Personal WRITING

Family WRITING

Home and School

*"One thing I learned early in my career
is that if you wait for the perfect
mood, or the perfect place or
the perfect situation, you'll
never write a word."*

—JOHN NICHOLS

This book is an introduction to the novel concept of family writing.

The ability to frame ideas in writing is an important skill that is greatly enhanced when it is valued and celebrated in the family. Much emphasis has been placed on the importance of families reading with their children, and we know that this practice helps children learn to read more easily. We don't talk about families writing together as being important to raising children who write well. When families write together from the time children are young, writing can become as important as reading. It becomes a natural activity, exerting its power for a lifetime.

The practice of writing is undergoing rapid change. We have largely abandoned the great historical exercise of letter writing. How few personal notes now enter our mailboxes! We use e-mail to send brief, often poorly constructed messages that are rarely saved as a history for future generations to read. Many are abandoning spelling in favor of the acronyms of the online chat room. Cursive writing is being replaced by printing. Composition is either avoided or turned over to professional writers.

Cell phones and cheap long-distance rates often seem to make writing unnecessary. Turning our society toward writing is a huge task. How can we make it happen?

We can start with ourselves. The family unit is small and able to affect change more quickly than society as a whole. Encouraging families to write together is one way to keep personal writing alive.

Does any of this matter? *Simply Write* is an attempt to convince you that indeed it does. But first, since the views expressed here come largely from my own experience, it is important that you know who I am and the credentials I bring to my work.

Above all else, I am a teacher. Teaching has been the consuming passion of my life. My career in the education system spanned twenty-nine years and covered grades one to nine. Since then I have been focusing on writing, presenting workshops on reading and writing, and teaching adults how to become effective reading coaches. Seeing parents struggling to help their children learn to read, and watching children give up in frustration at not being able to read, led to my first book, published in 1995. *Reading is More than Phonics: A Parents' Guide for Reading with Beginning or Discouraged Readers,* has become a bestseller. It has since been revised and published under the name *Simply Read: Helping Others Learn to Read.*

One of the highlights of my life was being selected as a charter member of the Calgary Writing Project. Teachers from grades one to twelve were chosen to participate in a university class based on the Montana Writing Project. The underlying philosophy of the project was that teachers of writing must write. And we wrote! We shared ideas, edited each other's writing and presented workshops. I remember the joy when I produced a piece that inspired a colleague to say, "That's great writing!" The Writing Project experience transformed the way I taught, and my personal writing took on new depth and flavor.

As a result of this training, I envisioned a conference where elementary and junior high students could come together in the same format as adults. The first Calgary Young Writer's Conference was held in 1981 with more than 1,000 participating students. They chose from a series of workshops led by authors, illustrators and storytellers. It was an impressive celebration of writing, and the conference is still a popular event in Calgary every spring.

As my hand flowed across the early pages of this manuscript, I knew instinctively what its most important message would be — the same message I gleaned from the Writing Project. If children are to learn how to write effectively and to fall in love with the process, they must see the adults in their lives writing.

My two most important roles in life have been as a parent and as a teacher. When I think about ways to improve writing, I reflect from both perspectives. My first audience in this book is parents. I particularly want to encourage parents to engage in family writing. For my second audience, teachers, I have tried to make suggestions that will enhance teaching as well as support families who want to honor writing in a new way. My third audience is everyone. We all need to feel confident about writing down our stories.

In the end, I decided to divide the book into three parts. Part I is dedicated to personal writing. Part II is devoted to family writing. Part III shows parents and teachers how they can work together to raise competent writers.

As I worked on an early draft of this manuscript I asked myself the question, "Why do I write?" I write because it gives me a clearer view of life and of my relationships with others. I write because it helps me read with understanding. I write for me. If some of it escapes to be of value to others, that is a bonus. I have to think of my own welfare first, just as in an airplane I have to first put on my own oxygen mask so that I am capable of helping someone else.

Writing takes time. Like many parents, you may think you can't possibly squeeze yet another activity into your already frantic family life. Nevertheless, I hope that as you read the following pages you will become convinced that celebrating personal writing in the family is indeed important to us as individuals, and to our society as a whole.

Acknowledgements CREDITS

This book was influenced by many people who crossed my path during the eighteen months or so that it took to write and produce. When people heard that I was writing about writing, many told me stories that helped shape my thoughts. I am eternally grateful to everyone who agreed to let me share their stories, and as a result breathed additional life into the work. It would have been difficult, perhaps even impossible, to clarify my ideas without them.

Rod Chapman of Knowledge Navigators and Elizabeth Collins Oman, my capable editors, helped enormously in the presentation of these ideas. Throughout the editing stages they challenged me to become a better writer, in the process making my voice stronger and adding urgency to my message about the importance of personal and family writing.

Gail Pocock of Bulldog Communications again used her considerable artistry to take the raw manuscript and turn it into a great-looking finished product. Gail worked on my first book, and she continues to have great faith in me and my message. Brian Hades of Edge Science Fiction Publishing wisely advised me on how to write copy for the cover and inside ads.

Special thanks to those who read my manuscript, gave invaluable feedback, and helped me in so many other ways: Lois Abbott, Frieda Boukall, Heather Buchwitz, Farhana Rendall Dhalla, Kimberly Edmonds, Marg Edmonds, Georgina Forrest, Liz Hagerman, Joy Hammersla, Pat Hogan, Luise Kinsman, Linda Parrington, Terry MacKenzie, Lorna Selig, Rae Sharpe, Jody Skinner, Morag Sparrow, Diane Thomas-Castle, and Linda Weir.

Dr. Bill Washburn, my mentor in the Calgary Writing Project, gave me sound advice in the early stages of this manuscript.

My family encourages me to follow my dreams. Thanks to Cathy, Susan and Peter, Judy and Jamie, for believing I can make a difference.

Personal
WRITING

WRITING ENRICHES OUR HUMANITY. It enables us to live with greater awareness, to make more sense of our lives. Personal writing lets us examine our inner selves in a different way. It helps us capture our thoughts so they can be remembered and absorbed. Personal journals form an incredible map of our journey through life — they become part of history. As Pulitzer Prize-winning author Tracy Kidder says, "I write because I don't know what I really think about anything until I get it down on paper."

Writing is for
EVERYONE

"As you begin to pay attention to your
own stories... you will enter into the
exciting process of becoming...
the creator of your own possibilities."

—MANDY AFTEL

Writing, like reading and speaking, is what makes us human.

Three recent experiences sharpened the message of this chapter for me: writing is not just for a chosen few individuals, writing is for you, me and everyone.

AT A SHOW CALLED *Once Upon a Time,* the Calgary Philharmonic Orchestra and Dave Kelly, host of The Big Breakfast television show, performed eight stories. The authors were children aged seven to twelve whose stories had been chosen from over 300 entries in a story-writing contest. It was delightful. Everyone was entranced by the humor and suspense created through the combination of reading and music. What a unique way to celebrate children's writing!

A DAILY RITUAL performed by many prairie farmers in the winter months is to meet for coffee in the local café. I had the privilege of joining a group of them in Saskatchewan recently. I was fascinated by their stories and their often heated reflections on society and politics as they bantered back and forth. When I inquired if any of these stories were being written down, they laughed and said that they weren't writers. How sad! Embedded in their animated story-telling were the intimate details that would greatly enrich a history of farming in the early twenty-first century in Western Canada.

THE MUSTARD SEED, a ministry for street people in Calgary, offers creative writing courses. I had the good fortune to spend time with Kathy after she began writing as a result of this training. Kathy battles mental illness and other difficulties but her life has greatly improved since she started to write. She says that writing has given her the confidence to try to put her life back together.

I loved the excitement in her voice as she told me how writing has helped her to look at her world differently. When she is angry, for instance, she writes two or three poems and her anger is gone. On bad days, however, when she says it would be helpful to write, she often doesn't feel like doing it. We laughed as she told me about being given a journal covered with handmade paper that is so beautiful she doesn't want to spoil it with writing. For years I, too, refrained from writing in a journal I was given because it was covered with soft handmade paper!

Kathy is now a reporter for The Mustard Seed's *Street Talk* newspaper, and she is a member of Speech Crafters, a Toastmasters club operated by the ministry. She says this is helping her, finally, to be able to look people in the eye. She has already spoken on behalf of street people at a major function. Writing has been the key to her progress. Looking back, she identifies one pivotal event that raised her self-esteem and is helping her to cope better with her life. Someone introduced her by saying, "This is Kathy. She is a writer." Here is an excerpt from one of Kathy's poems:

I disappear into the silence of nothingness.
No one even notices I'm missing, no one even cares.
I sail away in a ship that no one even sees.

It vanishes even from my sight.

Shall I ever return to shore? Or shall I watch from a far away place?

I get glimpses of your reality, quite different from mine

I know not a reality free from pain and confusion

I know not a reality of stability and here and now

The most I can ever hope for is a lessening of sailing

Not to feel confused or disoriented would be ideal.

STORIES HELP US LIVE OUR SONG

Each of us is a song in progress. We sing our songs in the way we conduct our lives. Our songs give us energy, power and reason for being. Storytelling records the notes, phrases and cadences. Sometimes our songs are full and beautifully melodious; sometimes they are sad and softly minor; occasionally they are loud, angry and boisterous — but they are always unique.

Your song will never be duplicated, so it is worthy of recording. I find my song in helping others become successful readers, in writing, in public speaking and in social interaction. Communicating with others makes me feel healthy, intelligent, witty and sensual. Where do you find your song?

By recording otherwise fleeting thoughts and re-reading your own writing, you learn about yourself. Personal writing lets you talk to your inner self; to discover your strengths. It is a powerful way to engage in more realistic self-talk.

We are most successful in helping others when we enable them to feel powerful and worthy. One of the greatest joys I experienced as a teacher was to watch the development of song in students as they became confident writers. I remember with delight the day a Grade Two boy read his little story to me. I praised him, assuring him that he was becoming quite a writer. "I know," he said eagerly, "I'm trying to decide whether to be a writer or a policeman when I grow up."

EVERYONE CAN WRITE

It takes determination. Seeds of doubt and discouragement tell us that we can't write, or that we don't have anything to write about, or that we don't have time to write. Root out these thoughts. We can all become writers. The material is there, we just have to clear away the obstacles. Many of us have to overcome the feelings of inadequacy about ourselves as writers that we have built up. We may still carry memories of low grades and bad experiences with writing from our life at school.

If you have the ability to form letters into words, you have everything you need. Just start where you are. Start by writing about your surroundings, what you love, hate, regret, celebrate or choose to spend time doing. Investigate why these things are important to you. Write about how they can be stepping-stones to an even fuller life.

Writing must become infectious, lively, energetic, imperfect, not fancy but what feels loose, easy, human, emotional. We tell our stories all day long. But they are like the bread crumbs that Hansel and Gretel dropped to mark their way through the woods. Unless they are written down, they disappear and are forgotten.

Becoming a writer requires two qualities that are free and available to everyone: *commitment and time.* We find time for the things we enjoy and value. To discover the joy of writing, we must steal time from other activities. This might even mean reducing the time we spend reading. Reading is enjoyable. It can consume so much time that there is none left for writing. Someone told me the other day that the only way he got started writing was to forbid himself to read a book for two weeks, and to spend the time he gained writing.

What is written is not as important as the act of writing itself. Writing provides a springboard for new ideas. Unlike speech, it can be revisited, revised and rewritten.

As you read this book, stop for a moment. Decide to commit a few minutes on a regular basis at whatever time suits your lifestyle. I'm best when I first wake up. But I find myself jotting down ideas throughout the day as new insights, vivid descriptions or apt sentences come to mind. I don't write every day. The important thing is to make the commitment, and to follow through by writing regularly.

I share G. Lynn Nelson's sentiment when he says in *Writing and Being,* "My wish for you is to be a lifelong writer. My hope is that writing will be a tool — an emotional, intellectual and spiritual tool — to help you survive and grow and find meaning and purpose and peace in your life."

RELAX! KEEP IT SIMPLE

JEFF WAS A HANDSOME YOUNG GOLF PRO who read poorly. I showed him how to read quickly and fluently by applying the principles of golf to reading. In return he gave me a wonderful gift, the book *Golf is Not a Game of Perfect* by Bob Rotella. I've played two games of golf in my life and they were both disasters for those playing with me. But the advice about becoming an excellent golfer has so much in common with excellence in reading that it helped me understand the dynamics of reading in a new way.

Rotella has plenty to say that applies to writing as well. He says that people are surprised by the simplicity of what he tells them. There is nothing mysterious, just good common sense. It is about learning to think in the most effective, efficient way possible; about having the confidence to try. He says, "My job as coach of mental skills is to help players go where they might not be able to go on their own, given their old ways of thinking." He contends that at least half the battle for golfing success occurs in the golfer's mind.

The block that keeps most people from writing is also in the mind. Because many people view writing as a gift given to a chosen few, they don't choose to write. But we can all write if we decide to do it. Like every other human endeavor it involves effort, but the more often we choose to write the better we get, and the writing will become easier and more pleasurable.

VISUALIZE SUCCESS

Great coaches, parents and teachers provide the type of support that enables participants to form mental images of success. By drawing attention to progress, no matter how small, we can praise and support the efforts of young writers until they are able to visualize what it feels like to perform well.

Writing involves recognizing and tapping the power within, and letting the words flow loosely onto the page. Joyce, who spends a lot of time golfing, told me a story that illustrates this beautifully. One of the golf courses she plays has a wide gully. For many years she stopped and prepared for what she found to be a difficult shot — and one that she rarely made. One day she said to herself, "Why am I doing this? If that was a field of grass I would just take a normal shot." From that day on she was usually able to hit her ball across the gully.

It is the same with writing. Excellence starts with a desire to communicate, and with thought pictures that visualize successful performance. Relax. Just write regularly and with confidence.

WRITING FORCES FOCUS

Writing a book is an incredibly rich learning experience for the author. When people discovered I was working on a book about writing, they told me their stories. I loved it and have re-told a number of their tales, with permission, in this book. On a recent flight I had the opportunity to swap stories with Terry, a marine biologist, who was on his way to work in the Arctic Ocean. He told me how he has spent his life doing scientific writing and reports. But when a series of events led him to become involved in a therapy group, he was asked to do personal writing. He was nervous. To his surprise, as he began to write, new ideas crowded into his mind and he found himself writing copiously.

Terry now finds personal writing to be a powerful tool. He shared with me his insight about why he thinks this is so. "When I have to physically write one word after the other on a page it is only possible if I focus on whatever I am writing about. It forces me to consider only the issue at hand."

How simple and how profound! Writing forces focus. I had never thought of it in that way before. Thanks, Terry, for helping me to understand the power of writing.

WRITING IS ITS OWN REWARD

I WAS TUTORING DUSTIN, a 10-year-old boy, in reading. His mother would give him treats after his lesson as a reward for paying attention. One day I talked to Dustin and his mother. "Reading is its own reward," I said. "When you are able to read *Where the Red Fern Grows* by yourself, Dustin, you will be so happy. I don't want you to get any more treats for reading." At Christmas he gave me a box of chocolates (with a few chocolates missing) accompanied by a handwritten note: To Mrs. Goodman. Reading is its own reward. Dustin.

Writing, the joy of creation, is its own reward too. Something about writing connects us more intimately with our subjects. When we begin to look closely at scenes, people or objects, they take on new dimensions and meaning. Writing about the people we meet takes relationships to a deeper level. I love the times when I decide to re-read my journal entries. Recalling special people who have influenced my life reminds me to keep in contact.

Thoughts are fleeting and difficult to capture — sometimes big ideas come in complete, beautiful sentences but if we don't write them down immediately they are gone, never to be recaptured with the same clarity.

Committing our impressions to paper makes them concrete. It lets us live the unique story of our lives with a sense of awareness that can't be achieved in any other way. We become more conscious of our choices, and of the results of our choices. In re-reading our own writing we can revisit events and learn from them in ways that totally escape us when we live only in an oral mode.

My friend, Marg Edmonds, who has an uncanny knack of giving me the right book at the right time, presented me with a copy of Julia Cameron's wonderful book, *The Right to Write: An Invitation and Initiation into the Writing Life.* Julia says writing will flourish when we focus "not on writing, but on life." We live life on so many levels and present different faces depending on the situation we are in and the people we are with. When we engage in personal writing our many personalities surface, giving our writing depth, perspective, vitality and incredible human interest.

Julia Cameron provides many worthwhile exercises to inspire writing. I decided to try her suggestion to go out by myself and to record my impressions in detail. I went for a walk at night and came back to write a descriptive piece that was different from anything I had ever attempted. Here is part of that journal entry:

> I just came from a wonderful walk. It is February, still winter but head-uncovered warm tonight. Tiny white snowflakes fall, invisible except in the light from the street lamp. The particles disappear into my silver hair and cluster in the twigs of the hedges. Given enough time, they will form thick blankets that cover the sidewalks and cling to the evergreens, decorating them with sparkles in the morning sun. I'm inside now. I am blessed to be here in this moment. Fire flickering in the fireplace assures warmth. Rod Stewart sings softly about the glowing moon and the fullness and comfort of being loved. I feel strong in this place.

Writing is indeed its own reward!

Summary of Key POINTS

WRITING *let's me talk to my inner self.* • *Writing is a vital part of being* **HUMAN**. • *It helps us* **DISCOVER** *our unique song.* • *We can become more aware by paying* **ATTENTION** *to our own stories.* • *Writing forces us to focus thought.* • *Writing captures precious* **MEMORIES**. • *All of life's experiences can be enriched with writing.* • *Visualize what* **SUCCESS** *will look like.* • *In unexpected ways writing* **REWARDS** *us.*

Writing as **S**elf **D**ISCOVERY

*"Let go of everything when you write.
Try, with simple words, to express
what you have inside."*

—NATALIE GOLDBERG

Writing gives thoughts and feelings a voice.

LISA PHONED ME IN A PANIC early one Monday morning. She was upset over the miserable Sunday their family had experienced because her twelve-year-old son was totally impossible all day. Fortunately, I keep an extra journal on hand. I asked her to come and get it and to write, in as much detail as possible, everything everyone said and did on Sunday. She replied, "But I said some terrible things!" I urged her to be honest because no one else needed to see it. She wrote six pages. It helped her to see the event more clearly and to gain insights into how changing her behavior might have improved the day. Here is an excerpt from Lisa's journal:

> His assignment is due tomorrow and all his stalling really
> gets me aggravated. The extra long shower, the Lego creation
> to build, time on the computer, snacks right after lunch.
> It always seems to be my job to get him started. He has more

delay tactics than I have motivational strategies. Shortly after starting his project his frustration level climbed to the point of tears. All the emotion seems to get in the way of actually accomplishing something. When he rejected my suggestion I lashed out with a sarcastic comment. I could see he felt diminished by my comment. I felt guilty and totally frustrated. I can see that I am having trouble letting go and letting him fall if necessary. It is so easy to see when someone else is being controlling. It is not so easy to admit that I'm doing it myself.

TALKING TO OURSELVES

How often have you listened to friends pour out their thoughts? You may have said little and given no advice, just provided a listening ear, an audience, but at the end they thanked you for how helpful you had been! Conversing about one's life is the basis of therapy.

Conversations with yourself through writing can be just as therapeutic. It sorts out ideas in strange ways. Relaxing and just writing thoughts as they arise can generate an amazing discussion that has surprising clarity.

When you have issues with others about how you have been treated, or about mistakes in judgment you have made, write about the issue putting in as much detail as possible. Think carefully about what happened. Then, when it is all written down, mentally give ownership of the problem to the person to whom it belongs, and release it from your own mind. If your writing turns up things you need to deal with, deal with them.

We all hope that we will learn from our mistakes. Personal journals that we don't have to show anyone give us confidence to write it down when we goof up. Analyzing more concretely what really happened helps us make more informed choices. When we re-read our stories, even years later, we realize how much we have grown in wisdom or, as is often the case, how little we have changed. Being able to revisit events through writing serves to bring life to a more conscious level where we can deal with it.

The added benefit is that we can read it again tomorrow and many years from now. Entries become a remarkable map of our journey. We can gain new strength and energy when we re-read the depressing parts. If we were able to overcome despair, fear, loneliness, indecision or bad judgment then, we can do it again now.

Writing is more than a form of communication with others. The process of writing opens the door to our inner being. Recording the conversations we have with ourselves helps us sort out why we think the way we do. When we write, we get to know ourselves more intimately, become more fluent and expressive, and live life more purposefully and with increased vitality. The process of writing things down sparks ideas and connections that lead to new discoveries about our real selves.

We do not have to be authors to write. Ernest Hemingway, the great novelist, once remarked that we are all apprentices in a craft where no one ever becomes a master. It is encouraging to know we can all be writers. Only some of us become novelists, poets or journalists.

SORTING EMOTIONS

LINDA HAD JUST BEEN THROUGH breast cancer surgery. When she discovered the cancerous lump in her breast, she determined to start a journal. After one entry, she quit. She said she didn't know what to write about. It might have helped Linda to write about what effect her discovery had on a specific family member or to record the wide variety of advice she received from well-meaning friends. Later, when Linda gave herself permission to record only one sentence a day, if that was all that came to her, she was able to write.

Sometimes it is important to write and edit a short piece until it precisely expresses an emotion or situation with just the right words. In *Free Play,* Stephen Nachmanovitch talks about the subtle awareness attained by playing the violin softly, and listening. Writing softly and listening to determine if we have really captured the essence of our feelings is a powerful experience. An example of this is when Mary writes to her stepchildren.

MARY TRIED TO REASON with her stepchildren but it often ended up in an emotional display that damaged rather than helped build good relations. She decided that instead of attempting to discuss the situation, she would write letters to them. They each agreed to give her a written response. It was a win-win situation for everyone. Mary saw herself and her role in the problem more clearly, and it gave the children time and space to consider solutions without the emotional overtones. When things went well, notes and cards of commendation were exchanged. The climate of their home improved dramatically and Mary provided the children with a model they could use for a lifetime.

Writing separates the writer from the recipient. It provides time for reflection and review, giving everyone the ability to handle situations more objectively.

OVERCOMING GRIEF

JAMES WAS COMPLETING his practicum for a Bachelor of Social Work. He was working with me under a mentorship program for children in high-needs schools. Cassy was a seven-year-old girl whose twenty-seven-year-old mother had just died from a drug overdose. No one could get Cassy to speak.

My advice to James was to meet with Cassy three times a week to create a book about an interesting topic such as bears, clowns, jungles, whatever. So he did. He read books to her to build background.

He wrote down ideas that they could use for their book. He just kept talking. Three weeks into this activity, Cassy started to respond. James was able to use his training in social work to counsel her in a wonderfully natural, effective way.

The principal reported that he was overcome when he saw Cassy skipping down the hall with a smile on her face. Cassy was suddenly talking again! Her grandfather was excited too, and came to the school to ask what had happened. Reading and writing together had enabled James and Cassy to establish a silent bond that engendered trust.

SORROW OVER STORIES LOST

As I was writing this book, I looked through a number of old files labeled 'My Writing.' A few pages of anecdotes from my years of teaching grade one caught my attention. After many years in upper elementary and junior high school and a stint in administration, I had asked for a placement in a grade one class in a high-needs school. I wanted to experience the joy of working with beginners, and to test the application to young readers and writers of the innovative teaching methods I had developed with older students.

I should have kept a daily journal during this exciting time of research and discovery. But I had large classes and I was extremely busy. All that survived were memories and scanty, random notes. My memory is weak and notes hastily penciled on whatever was at hand do not serve to give an adequate ongoing picture of the events and details of that time. Many of the little successes and failures that shaped our individual lives are long gone.

What a loss! Those two years were among the most successful of my entire teaching career. Now, looking back, how I would cherish the details of the struggles and victories I shared with the delightful youngsters in my classes. I do remember one humorous story, probably because it was an ego-booster.

As THE STUDENTS GATHERED on the rug one morning for sharing time, some of the girls began telling me that they liked my dress, my earrings, etc. Jimmy, a small scruffy boy with a perpetually runny nose, listened to the gushy girls. Not to be outdone he said, "Mrs. Goodman, I like everything about you!" What priceless jewels they were.

WRITING STORES THOUGHT

We may have all the glorious ideas and insights in the world, but if they are not written down they are often lost. We are unable to use them to positively affect our own lives or the lives of others.

Writing gives thoughts and feelings a voice. Writing from who we are, from the inside, is always right. It can never be judged.

Novelists, poets and journalists string words together to produce inspiring or thoughtful works, sometimes even masterpieces. In the same way, gifted speakers entertain and inspire large audiences. Does that stop the rest of us from speaking?

Writing is a powerful form of therapy.

Summary of Key POINTS

WRITING is a conversation with oneself. • It is a powerful form of **THERAPY**. • Writing sorts out **EMOTIONS** unemotionally. • Writing thoughts on paper creates an opportunity for **REFLECTION** and review. • The process starts with the **DESIRE** to try. • It results in increased self-confidence. • Thoughts and feelings are given a **VOICE** with writing.

Writing

HISTORY

"I am a great believer in going back to original documents... the strongest underpinnings for a book."

—PIERRE BERTON

Every story of a life lived is history.

IRENE WAS A FASCINATING WOMAN who had lived a full life, replete with many stories interesting enough to be the subject of a novel. When Irene became bedridden with cancer her daughter, Marion, hired a professional writer to record those stories. No one realized the importance of recording her story until it was almost too late. I asked Marion why she hadn't written about her mother herself. "I'm not a writer," she replied.

MARION IS AN INTELLIGENT, talented woman. She and her husband have spent a lifetime coaching cross-country skiing, running a helicopter skiing company and operating a kayaking business in the Queen Charlotte Islands. She has the ability to write her mother's stories, not to mention those from her own exciting and challenging life. Later, when Marion realized how much she valued the stories of her mother's life produced by the professional writer, she started to record her own adventures.

MY NINETY-YEAR-OLD MOTHER was widowed at forty-two and has lived a life of service to others that is worthy of recording. Only recently have I begun to write her story. Marion and I have been writers all along, but we have fallen for the mistaken notion that only some people have the special gift to be writers.

WHAT'S AT STAKE?

Societies and religions that have valued and spawned writers have had the most influence on the direction in which humanity has progressed. When we fail to write down our stories, bits of history are lost for all time. "History repeats itself," we say. When events are recorded and read, we have an opportunity to learn from our predecessors.

Democracy is based in writing even more strongly than in speaking. Speeches influence partly because of voice, gesture and inflection. Writing is more grounded, capable of being read, digested and contemplated. It informs us on a different level. A society that loses or silences its writers can no longer function as a democracy that depends on reading and writing to make informed choices.

The Diary of Samuel Pepys, written in the seventeenth century, have become well known because they are the only information we have about life during the period in which he lived. The details of Anne Frank's life as recorded in her diary keep alive the humanity of the holocaust. History is not just about the events that seem to be important to society as a whole. History is the everyday life of everything on our planet — human, animal and plant life included.

One day I received a long letter from Elsie. What an unusual treat! I rarely find a handwritten letter in my mailbox any more. She reminisced on our forty years of friendship, and quoted passages she knew would interest me from the book she was reading. I felt warm and special as I read. Tears came to my eyes. Someone had taken the time to write a letter to me. It is now stored with my important papers!

PERSONAL STORIES ARE HISTORY

We underestimate the value of our stories. Everyone has unique, interesting stories to tell and we do so in conversation every day. But most of them are never written down. Start writing a story about an event in your childhood, or about an unusual incident at work, or about an interesting celebration you attended. Put in lots of drama and colorful words. Stretch the truth just a little! No one will know or care. If it helps, tell the story into a tape recorder and listen to it before writing. Read the story to your family. They will love it.

Personal stories have unlimited potential. Encourage grandparents, aunts, uncles, cousins and friends to write their stories and to send them to your family. It's easy to do these days as an attachment to an e-mail.

Women seem more inclined than men to keep journals, yet men delight in swapping stories and have exciting personal stories to share. We can encourage them by recording their stories and putting them into print. With permission, record friends and family when they are telling stories informally. It is often easier to tell a colorful story in a group than to write it down. Put the best ones into a short-story collection. Your friends will be pleased to receive copies. The stories might even be good enough to publish. Print-on-demand companies make it easy and inexpensive to turn personal writing into books.

Parts of our history are ours, and ours alone. We need to know that our journals are private. A pledge must be made not to read another's journal without permission. This encourages honest writing about feelings and incidents not suitable for sharing. Some people have two journals and keep the personal one locked or hidden.

GROWING OUR ROOTS

Native American history illustrates the powerful role of story in forming cultural identity, and in building a framework for individuals to achieve a sense of self-worth.

RUPERT ROSS, A JUDGE IN NORTHERN CANADA, spent three years examining the widespread aboriginal preference for 'peacemaker justice.' He wrote an enlightening book, *Returning To The Teachings,* in which he recalls Basil Johnston's discussion, in *Ojibway Heritage,* of the traditional way natives raised children to be responsible adults. Theirs was an oral tradition. They provided the children with an endless supply of stories, rather than endless lists of do's and don'ts. "To foster individuality and self-growth, children and youth were encouraged to draw their own inferences from the stories. No attempt was made to impose upon them views."

It seems to me that native children forced into residential schools lost the stories that would have given them an understanding of their traditional way of life — an understanding that would help them in their adult life. Instead, they were faced with a huge emphasis on do's and don'ts, and on stories from a foreign culture. They grew up without the stories that could give their own children roots.

For thousands of years in native culture, relationships with nature, animals and humans (in that order) were more important than rules. This way of looking at life was passed on through story. This is a complete reversal of our western way of thinking.

How difficult it will be for aboriginal leaders to re-establish this philosophy. For this generation, it is critical that mothers and fathers write down as many family stories from grandparents as possible — before the stories die with them.

HERITAGE WRITING

Ethnic and cultural stories reflect the history of a nation. The ongoing history of every nationality needs to be recorded for future generations. It is easy for immigrants to get caught up in the stories of their new environment. But written and recorded family stories from their countries of origin will enchant subsequent generations, and provide information that would otherwise be forgotten. Stories, written in whatever language is easiest, could include myths, legends and events from the life that was lived before the family immigrated.

How I would treasure the details of my grandparent's lives as pioneers, or my father's experiences on the long ocean voyage he undertook when he immigrated to Canada. If only they had realized the importance of writing it down. If only I had understood how much I would later wish that I had written their stories down.

Because Writing Matters, a book sponsored by the National Writing Project in the United States, describes how the International High School in New York State uses first languages to start teenage immigrants writing, even before they are proficient English speakers.

"All new students are paired with a student of the same first language so they can help each other by using their native language. Students work collaboratively." By arranging for students to meet in groups to discuss ideas in the language they have thought in all their lives, writing achieves a clarity that would be impossible in English only.

The school is conducted around themes. Emphasis is placed on making connections between themes and content across disciplines. For example, three-dimensional temples using mathematical concepts learned in science class were constructed after students wrote about mythology for their humanities class.

The school discovered that, "Students take responsibility for their learning when they need to write about it."

READING BECOMES HISTORY

We learn by living with ourselves, and with others. We learn a lot when we live with the characters in a book. As we follow their progress, we assimilate bits of their lives into our own. I write something in my journal about every book I read. I copy strong passages and write about the memories, reflections and the emotions they inspire. Understanding is reinforced in ways never accomplished by reading alone.

Reading becomes infinitely more instructive and memorable when we write about it. The resulting awareness makes us able to chart a more vivid life and to engage in more interesting conversations with others. An added benefit is that writing comments and quotes about the books we read records an important history. We are a product, not only of our conversations and experiences, but of the books and other written material we read. Writing about the ideas, events and characters that enter our lives through reading not only enriches our own experience, but gives us material to use when we write creative stories.

A re-read of my journals brings the books and my reflections to life again, even long after I have forgotten about them. Here is an example of one of my journal entries:

My next read is *Wherever You Go There You Are*. That's an intriguing title. I just finished reading *Hanna's Daughters*. After Hanna dies, her daughter Anna declares, "I will never return here again." Anna may not return but even if she does it will never be the same. When I re-visit any situation, it is always new. Circumstances around it have changed. I have changed. Anna's comment and the title of this new book may be saying the same thing. Wherever we go we carry the totality of our past experience, no matter how hard we try to leave it behind.

History is a record of all the things that shape us.

Summary of Key POINTS

Writing records the personal **DETAILS** of history.

• **DEMOCRACY** depends on writing. • Writing preserves cultural identity. • It **INFORMS** and delights future generations. • History is everyday life. • We are all **STORYTELLERS** in our daily lives. • Writing stories down ensures that they will survive. • **LEARNING** is reinforced with writing. • Reading is more **MEMORABLE** when it is accompanied by writing.

Writing and SPELLING

"Writing is simply about the desire to tell a story. An editor can always correct your spelling and fix your grammar but only you can tell your story."

—FANNIE FLAGG

Writing and the mechanics of writing must not be confused.

TONY WAS A DELIGHTFUL eleven-year-old boy, intelligent, compassionate and caring. At Christmas he went shopping on his own and carefully selected an appropriate Christmas card for each of his teachers. He loved to write imaginative stories which he sent to his grandparents. He was an avid reader.

When Tony entered grade six things changed. Normally a happy boy, he became depressed, nervous and anxious. He was subjected to many tests at school and his parents were asked to get an IQ test, a psychologist's report, an eye test and a hearing test. What was the source of the despair that descended on this family?

Tony couldn't spell.

Despite the fact that he and his parents worked diligently on the weekly spelling list, he continued to fail tests. He labeled himself dumb.

How ridiculous! Failing because he couldn't perform what had become impossible for him at this time in his life. All the testing in the world would not make him a better speller. He needed a break.

There are many Tonys for whom spelling is a huge burden. The inability to spell well can become a stumbling block to writing. One of the goals of this book is to separate these two important skills — the ability to spell and the ability to write.

In *Simply Read* I make the case that effective readers rarely use vowels to read. They make sense of text using as few letters as possible. As a reading coach, I used this principle to help many students become effective readers. Then I was asked to tutor spelling.

EIGHT-YEAR-OLD STEVEN, a non-reader, was referred to me for help. He had a brilliant mind and a remarkable facility with words. Teaching him to read was easy. Then his parents asked me to help him with spelling. Despite our best efforts, Steven couldn't distinguish between the short vowel sounds. The lack of consistency in spelling rules, combined with his inability to hear short vowels, made correct spelling an unachievable goal for Steven, at least at this early stage of his life. In a later conversation with his mother I learned that his inability to spell has been a huge emotional burden on Steven, and has hampered his success in school.

Teaching students of all ages has led me to realize that most children are not good at, or interested in, everything. Ross Greene in *The Explosive Child* puts it this way, "Some children — no matter how hard they and their parents, teachers and coaches try — are just not built to be great athletes... or spellers."

We value diversity in adults. Aren't you happy that some people are gifted mechanics, that accountants like to work with numbers, and that others can organize businesses so we have jobs? We appreciate the unique abilities of singers, artists, actors, storytellers and comedians. They make life colorful and worth living. Why do we label children as failures because they can't excel in all subjects?

MECHANICS AND WRITING

Spelling, grammar and the mechanics of writing are important. But achieving mastery over the punctuation depends on order and timing. Those who are firm in the belief that they are writers will try harder to master the tools of writing. Fostering a love of writing comes first.

In this book I celebrate writing as an improvisation freely created from the fabric of experience. I know that improvisation cannot occur without some skills. A quilter will not become a maker of exquisite quilts without first learning how to sew. A musician cannot create great music without learning how to play the instrument.

It is the same with writing. Beginning writers need to develop the basic skills with which to begin practicing their craft. They need to know, at the very least, how to form words and sentences. But we do these budding writers a great disservice when we focus our critique on their spelling.

When students bring home a piece of writing in draft form, we tend to focus on the spelling errors because they are so easy to spot. We may or may not get around to commenting on the ideas, or on the words and phrases that are particularly graphic, or on the quantity of writing that represents real effort.

Pause for a moment to think this through. Most students are not going to write in quantity if they know that they will have to correct everything. Nor will they choose to use large, colorful words if they are required to spell them correctly.

Writing is an art that crafts pictures with words. It takes only a pinch of unsolicited criticism to stop its flow. If we can resist judgment until learners have confidence, they will be more likely to accept constructive criticism. A good way to keep from commenting on mechanics in a story is to make it a practice to ask a question that extends the story or to find something to praise.

"Wow, what a neat character you created," or "I like the way you expressed that idea. I never thought of that before," or "I didn't realize that you could use such descriptive words," or "You painted a wonderful word picture of that desolate house for me. What an artist you are," or "I love the way you tricked me with that surprise ending," are examples of comments that will encourage young writers. Using comments such as these, we can help students experience the thrill and confidence that accompanies positive reinforcement.

We give time and effort to things we value, things that spark our interest, and things that offer the possibility of success. The best way to interest students in improving spelling is to help them become competent writers so they have a need to spell!

CHANGING TACTICS

At EIGHTY-FIVE YEARS OF AGE, Bob Jesson was looking for a young horse to train. The Cowboy Hall of Famer, inducted for his ability to school horses, especially horses that others have given up on, shared the secret of his success with me. "Go back to something the horse does well and praise his performance," said Bob. "Slowly introduce the things you want to improve, always watching for successful behaviors to praise, and the horse will soon be trainable."

Children are a lot like horses. We have to change tactics when things aren't going well. Failing day after day, especially before one's family, is unbearable and totally unconscionable. We need to back off, to remove concerns about the current obstacle, to rescue the child by assigning tasks that can be accomplished until confidence is restored. You can lead a horse to water but you can't make him drink. In the same vein, you can force a child to do activities, but he or she has to accomplish the learning individually.

Spelling lists are one of the most traditional activities of school and of homework. When I was speaking on writing at a conference of educators recently, some teachers shared that many students who do well on the weekly spelling lists show little carry-over to everyday spelling. I suggested that lists may not be the best way to teach spelling. It is difficult to find a list that challenges the good spellers while addressing the needs of those who are struggling. By the end of our conversation we agreed that lists aren't always effective and can cause unnecessary strain.

Maybe we can change our approach, at least for some children. There are other ways to learn to spell. Playing games that involve analyzing words is much easier and more effective than attempting to memorize words in isolation. Parents may be willing to donate games to build up a collection for the classroom. Students can play the games together at school to learn the rules. Occasionally, the games can be sent home as spelling homework. Playing word games together builds family relationships, creates an interest in words and develops the elusive sense all good spellers have that tells them when a word doesn't look right.

The sound of a word is not always a good guide to spelling it. More than thirty percent of the time, rules lead to incorrect spelling. Instead of relying on the rule book for spelling, encourage students to put a check mark beside words they aren't sure of, and to look them up later. Work on recognizing errors, which is easier on the brain than memorization.

Resources for alternate approaches to spelling and names of available games are included in the bibliography at the end of this book.

SPELLING GAMES AND ACTIVITIES

Thea Morris has written four excellent books for teachers that present creative ways to teach spelling. Parents, too, will discover ideas and games that encourage students to have fun while improving their spelling. For instance, they could adapt her suggestion that teachers have students "write about their feelings toward spelling, how they see themselves as spellers, or what they know about specific spelling strategies." Family members might write about spelling and then talk about the feelings they have toward it. If done before and after changing the approach to learning to spell, this could serve as an informative evaluation. I have adapted a game from Morris's most recent book *Spelling Rules — A Complete Spelling Program for Grades 1-3*. Here is a suggestion about how to play one of them:

CUT OUT LETTERS

MATERIALS:
Paper, glue, scissors, magazines, flyers, catalogs, newspapers.

INSTRUCTIONS:
Choose words from the weekly spelling list or use ten new words from reading. Players search for and cut out letters from the printed materials to spell each of the words. They glue the letters in the correct order on their individual papers. The player who has the most words at the end of a set time wins. If a player finds the complete word it is considered a bonus and is cut out and glued as is. Occasionally, make it more fun by giving extra points for the most creative page. Art work can be added at the end and the finished product displayed.

SPELLING CAN IMPEDE WRITING

When we are satisfied with the content, we can go back and correct the spelling. Students cannot write freely if they stop to get spelling help from a parent, a dictionary or the teacher. They may avoid using difficult words if they are required to spell them correctly in their first draft. When we stop writing, for any reason, we interrupt the flow of ideas coming into consciousness.

To become good writers, students must do lots of spontaneous writing — much of which sees only the garbage can. The great classic composer, Brahms, once remarked that the mark of an artist is in how much he throws away. We need to encourage children to write freely and help them to pick their best pieces for editing and polishing.

Arrange for celebrations of writing. If we know that others will read our writing it is more rewarding to work on spelling and mechanics. When we write for others, we owe it to our readers to edit. This ensures that we express ideas clearly and that spelling, punctuation and grammar are correct.

The story is told that when Margaret Atwood, a highly acclaimed Canadian novelist, informed her mother that she was going to be a writer her mother reminded her that it might not be a good choice because she couldn't spell. Margaret assured her mother that she could always get someone to spell for her.

WHAT ABOUT HANDWRITING?

In a conversation I had with a group of well-educated parents two surprising questions were posed. The first question was, "Is handwriting too difficult?" The second question was even more startling: "Is hand-writing important now that we have computers?"

I was shocked. I had never even entertained such questions. I always thought the ability to write quickly and legibly was an important skill despite the availability of computers.

Later I had the pleasure of becoming re-acquainted with Kyle, a brilliant young man whom I had known in kindergarten. We discussed writing by hand in a journal. He told me that he does all his writing on the computer because he can't write by hand anymore.

One of the more disturbing legacies of computers may be a decline in handwriting ability. Are we in danger of losing the fine art of handwriting? Does it matter?

I think it does. Handwriting, like spelling, is a face we show in public. Computers aren't always available. For many reasons, all students need to write by hand in school. Poor penmanship slows the writing process. It can also affect the way teachers grade papers. Handwriting may influence whether or not we are hired for a job. It is part of our personality. Although poor handwriting shouldn't deter us from personal writing, fluent handwriting certainly makes it easier.

Many young people hold their pencils in strange ways. This can result in an inability to write quickly and fluently. We are asking children to write much earlier than we did in the days when they started school in grade one. It is important for parents of young children and workers in daycares and pre-schools to help children hold their pencils and crayons properly. It can quickly become a habit that is almost impossible to change.

When I visited a grade one class at Aspen Heights School in Red Deer, I noticed how well the students held their pencils. I learned that the kindergarten teacher, Frieda, feels this is so important that she enlists the cooperation of parents as part of her intake interviews. Frieda asks them to have their children hold crayons or pencils with the thumb and third finger so that the index finger is free to make what she calls an 'alligator's mouth.' She gives students short pieces of chalk and breaks pencils in half so it is impossible to hold them the wrong way.

Facility with handwriting, spelling, punctuation and grammar and the ability to express thoughts quickly and clearly, all make writing easier — but in their absence, write anyway. Simply write in a way that feels good for you — don't worry about the audience. That can come later.

Confidence and desire are at the heart of writing.

Summary of Key POINTS

WRITING is an art that crafts pictures with words. • It is always a new creation. • Writing conveys a **MESSAGE**. • It is not dependent on correct spelling. • Focus on **CONTENT,** not spelling. • The structure and content of written words can be edited. • Changing **STRATEGIES** reduces stress. • Games are fun and make learning to spell easier. • **HANDWRITING** is important.

II

Family WRITING

WE NEED TO CREATE A SOCIETY that encourages all family members to write. There are many easy and practical ways to make authors of young children long before they are capable of actual writing. This builds the foundations for writing to become a lifelong, natural activity. By creating a community of writers, starting at the level of the family, we can strengthen our collective knowledge.

Writing can
START EARLY

*"Any subject can be taught
effectively in some intellectually
honest form to any child at any
stage of development."*

—JEROME BRUNER

Writing deserves the same attention as speaking and reading.

▬ Jerome Bruner, one of the best-known and most influential psychologists of the twentieth century, contends that learning must be based in the arousal of interest. His constant theme is that education is a process of individual discovery. He argues that we postpone the teaching of important subjects because they are deemed too difficult. We underestimate what young children are capable of learning.

Readiness is not only born but made. The most important time for brain development is during the first three years of life. Infants are able to understand much more than they can verbalize. To achieve maximum mental growth they need an environment rich in diversity, with lots of opportunities for learning new things. We should be talking to young children about everything they encounter, and reading to them from all kinds of fiction and non-fiction. If we treat children as responsible, contributing group participants, they will grow up that way.

ADULTS AS BRIDGE BUILDERS

Children have the innate ability to learn. It is the task of caregivers to build bridges for them to access knowledge within the family circle and in the outer world. Adults support and extend curiosity in children by treating them as more capable than they actually are.

When children are learning to speak, adults have remarkable sensitivity to their progress. The degree of overlap in the circles of adult and child conversations determines their success in becoming fully literate. The manner in which adults communicate with children helps them learn how to extend their speech into new contexts.

Thought comes into existence through words. Words represent knowledge. Children who hear a variety of words have an advantage in both reading and writing. The more different kinds of interactions they have with words, the more capacity they have for literate thought.

Adults mediate learning by formatting events in such a way that young learners are assisted in becoming accountable for their own learning. In his book, *Child's Talk*, Jerome Bruner defines format as "a standardized interaction pattern between an adult and child that establishes roles that eventually become reversible." These interactions generally have a playful, game-like nature. By helping young children to figure out things for themselves, adults build their self-image as learners and thus keep on the growing edge of the child's competence. The things you do together gradually become activities that children can do alone.

CREATE YOUR OWN BOOKS

You can't tell young children about the importance of writing, you can only help them discover the fun of it. We create a fictional world by engaging in dialogue that extends a story, setting the stage for children to create text. Reading a good book can serve as a catalyst for engaging in fantasy, creative dialogue, empathy, prediction, critical judgment and the analysis of personal relationships. Children can learn to write by being invited to be co-writers. After you have read and discussed a book, have your child retell the story. Write the child's own words down and create a little book. Ask questions during the retelling to extend the story and make it more interesting.

Creating books as part of reading time is fun and easy. All adults can do it. You don't have to be able to read or write well to make books with young children. Anyone can create a book based on a conversation with a child. An attractive picture book is an excellent stimulus for discussion and book-making, even if the text is not read. Have your child tell the story of the pictures and write it down exactly as it is told. After you read about an animal, create a story giving the animal human qualities.

Any non-fiction can serve as a stimulus for a book, and the making of books does not have to be restricted to stories. You can also write about trips taken, activities engaged in, or lessons you want to teach. Another idea is to take pictures of a favorite toy or pet at a shopping mall, a playground, a campsite or a formal dinner. Make up a story to go with the pictures and presto, another book! What fun!

Children know an enormous amount about stories long before they have the dexterity and skills to write. Capitalize on this knowledge by scribing for them, even well into later childhood. Older children might create books about sports or topics they are studying. It is a win-win; a reason for writing, and an appreciative audience.

ADD INTERESTING DETAILS

Many adults like to dabble in art and are very capable of illustrating the books. Children will be excited by your attempts and will not judge for quality. Family photos, collage materials and pictures from magazines can also adorn the pages. Give a young child's book to an older sibling to illustrate. Instead of printing the text for these early books, provide variety by cutting the words from magazines and newspapers and pasting them in. Find the words and arrange them on the page. Then your child can paste them on using a glue stick. Children will soon want to place the words themselves, and that can lead to another important discussion about design and balance.

Finish by giving the book a title and a cover with both the child's name and the illustrator's name on it. Do all of this as part of your play together. Whatever looks like play is taken seriously by children.

Writing has to become an important part of life from the beginning, just like reading. The simple act of sharing, and the satisfaction and fun encountered in making books together will propel your child's desire to write. It may even become a stimulus for the whole family to create books. Celebrating books in this way gives writing a positive place in the self-talk of children. You validate their creativity and approve of their intelligence by writing down their words.

Store the books in a special place where they can be easily accessed to show visitors. What treasures these books will be! They will be enjoyed for generations, and you will cherish the fond memories they generate. I wish I had made books that recorded the delightful language of my children and grandchildren when they were learning to talk.

Just as children learn by being read to that print has meaning, hearing their own language in a book teaches them that they too can make meaning through writing. They become authors before they know what the term means. When they become capable of writing for themselves, it is just an extension of an already-ingrained habit.

The skills and mechanics of writing are learned at school, but children who come to school with this writing and story-telling background already in place will be much more interested in becoming competent writers. If more parents celebrated writing from the beginning, our schools would greatly benefit.

Reed, a grade one student, wrote the following story as part of an ocean theme. It is a delightful story that could be turned into a four-page book. An example of how to use photographs to illustrate a children's book follows the story. Also included is a sample page from three-year-old Sam's retelling of *Goldilocks and The Three Bears* using illustrations and words cut from a magazine.

Reed's Story
My Shark and Me

my Shark

me and my Shark

Went for a Wac we

Wact to the Parc

and ges Wat we

Saw a octuPoos

we aSct if we can

PlaY he Sed YeS So

we PlaYd Win we

PlaYda bolYcam he Sed

bu groff

and we Sed No dee end

When we played a bully came. He said, "BUGGER OFF!" and we said, "NO."

The little wee **Bear** chased her **AND** she never saw anything again. The End

PARENTS AS EDUCATORS

It is widely accepted that parents are a child's first and most important teachers. School-based education alone cannot take the place of quality interaction with infants and young children within the home.

The research for my master's thesis looked at the roots of reading in the interactions between mothers and their just-turned-two daughters. It became evident as I worked with these mothers that the only effective and economical way to assure literacy for everyone was — and still is — to involve parents in the educational process while their children are still infants.

I used the classic book *Rosie's Walk* by Pat Hutchins as the basis for my research. It is an example of a book that can be used to inspire even a two-year-old to tell a story. What follows is my recording of one mother's conversation with her daughter, Katie, while reading the page with a picture of the fox just ready to leap on Rosie the hen.

Mother: Run, run! Hurry, tell Rosie to run!

Kate: Run, run! Hurry! Run Rosie and run and run around (waves arms as she talks).

Mother: Run so the fox won't get you. Whoa! Shew! He missed again!

Kate: Poor fox. (She rubs the page gently.) Poor fox. Poor fox.

Kate's mother could have followed up this reading by having Kate tell the story of the fox, or of Rosie, based on the exciting pictures in this book. She could create another story by talking about the farmyard, or what the farmer does, or where the fox lives, and so on. Each telling could be made into a little book of its own. It would be helpful to use this opportunity to find more books in the public library about foxes and hens. Every story can spark a multitude of other ideas to discuss. Imagination is all it takes.

DIALOGUE BUILDS INTELLIGENCE

The cornerstone of a child's development is social interaction. A young child builds thought processes based on what happens in interactions within the family, and between family and community. Learning results from cooperation between child and adult. The mind does not grow naturally, or unassisted. Early conceptual learning takes place through collaboration with an adult. Literate interchanges with others and the meaningful use of language becomes part of a child's brain development.

Research has shown that, regardless of social class, a caregiver who extends a child's talk and provides a variety of experiences is a major influence on literacy development. The child who receives frequent, quality dialogue with an adult develops the most rapidly. When reading and writing with children, it is important to choose the right books. The quality of a book can be judged by its ability to provoke the kind of dialogue that enriches experience and develops new vocabulary. To foster mental growth, the discussion that surrounds the book is even more important than the book itself.

In these discussions, the degree to which an adult can take the perspective of the child has a marked effect on the achievement of literacy. The most effective way to help children is to pay close attention to their talk, and to build on it without worrying about correctness.

Recording these interchanges in writing through books, poems, songs, posters or any other written medium is the easiest, most successful way to have all of this happen naturally. The parent's role is to create successful experiences that encourage the child to believe that writing is a worthwhile and pleasurable thing to do.

We speak for children until they can speak.

We read for children until they can read.

We need to write for children until they can write!

Summary of Key POINTS

WRITING *can become natural like speaking and reading.* • *Writing* **ENHANCES LIFE** *from the cradle to the grave.* • *Structured events mediate writing.* • *Writing may be* **ILLUSTRATED** *by someone else.* • *Writing with young children is a* **PLEASURABLE** *and worthwhile activity.* • *The basis for writing is rooted in reading and storytelling.* • *Writing is* **STRENGTHENED** *by interactive dialogue.* • *Early writing contributes to making writing a lifelong habit.*

Writing in the

FAMILY

"Writing is learned
by writing, by reading, and
by perceiving oneself
as a writer."

—FRANK SMITH

The roots of family life give shape to the tree.

Two elementary school boys from different families were studying with me to improve their writing skills. To encourage them, I presented journals to each member of both families and requested that they all begin to write. Rita and Larry's family was leaving for vacation in Hawaii and decided to take the journals and write while on holiday. The other family stayed in town but they, too, agreed to begin recording their activities.

Later, when the vacationers had returned, both families brought their journals to a potluck supper. What fun, as fathers, mothers and children all participated in this celebration of writing. The two younger girls had drawn pictures, and the adults had printed their stories. The whole experience was so enjoyable that they decided to do it again. Rita remarked on the value of having such concrete memories of their wonderful vacation in Hawaii. Here's an excerpt from Larry's journal:

Snorkeling gives you a feeling of flying like a bird over a strange land of mountains and sandy plains with smaller multicolored birds below. On a calm day with clear water you want to give chase to the other fish. After a few dives the pain in your ears reminds you that you are only a visitor.

A PINT OF EXAMPLE OR A GALLON OF ADVICE?

Children who see their parents writing, whether to record events, to sort out problems or to stimulate imagination, will grow up valuing writing. Acquiring the habit of writing when they are young increases the chance that they will later engage in the work necessary to become competent writers. When children see the adults in their lives writing, it delivers the unspoken message that writing is an important part of everyday life. We live in an increasingly oral and visual culture. Television, the Internet, cell phones and cheap long-distance rates all help connect us immediately with the whole world. Does this make writing less important as a form of communication? I would argue that writing has become even more important. For many, it is an essential skill. Everyone who works in our knowledge-based economy requires strong writing skills.

GETTING STARTED

Parents whose children are already in school may have lost the early opportunity to instill the tradition of family writing, but it is never too late to start. You may meet with resistance from older children who do not want to do extra writing. Writing takes time, and there is never enough time to go around. Your success will depend on holding a family meeting to discuss personal writing and why it is important. If everyone can see value in supporting each other by sharing writing, making a plan to find the time will be easier.

When your family has agreed to give this a try, look at the calendar to find a time when everyone can be together. Make it a priority. Assign a time frame, and try to stay within it. At the first session discuss what kind of support would be valuable, decide on a plan of action and set some goals. Have a variety of types of journals, notebooks and pens. Let each person choose which tools they like best. Making a choice is a small commitment to actually using them.

The first step to good writing is the ability to organize thoughts orally. Those who have spent a lot of time with video games, computers and television sometimes haven't had a lot of practice carrying on a conversation. One-way communication mediums do not teach children how to engage in dialogue. Personal stories, jokes and discussing interesting news events are ways to get a conversation going.

To get started, you might set aside one evening each week for discussion around the dinner table. Choose a topic for consideration.

SOME SOURCES ARE:

- current affairs, newspaper stories and magazine articles
- important family decisions that need to be made
- an interesting topic that one child is researching for school

If possible, frame some questions to guide the writing for the week. Everyone can write a few sentences about the chosen topic, and bring them to the next session. To get reluctant writers of all ages started, it might be helpful to give them the choice of taping comments. Someone in the family can volunteer to put them into writing. Family discussions around worthwhile topics greatly help students to succeed at school.

Nurture the beginnings of writing as you would a plant poking its first leaves from the ground. Start small and let it grow on its own. Encourage students of all ages to bring home their rough drafts from school. Find something good to praise, however small. Ask questions about parts that aren't clear. Make suggestions about the order of events. Just like movies, stories can begin at the end and go back to detail specific events. Talk about the importance of an inviting opening and a satisfying ending. Discuss content without commenting on spelling, handwriting or other mechanics.

PARENTS AS MODELS

Some parents may want to try modeling personal writing before introducing the concept of family writing. Write alone or in a favorite chair where everyone can see you. Choose five causes that you are interested in or five things you are thankful for. Pick one and record all the thoughts that come to you about it. Keep on recording your thoughts. Don't worry about how much you write, just quit when it seems you have no more to say. There is no right or wrong way. Just do it. Begin writing and ideas will come to you. This is especially important advice for fathers because it seems to me that boys need to see men writing.

Write about family and friends. Incorporate conversations, incidents and your own self-talk. Create characters in your mind until you can see them in detail. Place them in setting after setting. Let your subjects meet one character after another, some of whom come to visit and quickly depart, others who stay. Show how the characters experience the same joys and disappointments that are common to us all.

Write as an observer with field glasses that accentuate the details. Write about experiences as if you are an outsider looking at the situation. Give the participants different personalities; try to get into their shoes, to imagine what they would say.

Give some of your writing to your children to edit. It is great modeling and gives them a chance to analyze your writing for things they are being taught at school. We always learn best when we are teaching someone else. Don't miss this opportunity to discuss ideas and to solve composing problems together.

BUILDING VOCABULARY

Words are the building blocks of writing. We use experiences to explain experiences. We cannot speak or write outside of the words we possess. Writing is only exciting and informative if we have appropriate words at our disposal. Thinking can expand only as far as it has words to consider. Reading and writing are connected in this way. Many of the words used in writing are never used in normal conversation. We collect words by reading widely. One family told me that they choose a 'Word of the Week' that everyone tries to use as much as possible.

Be creative. Find a wall or create a bulletin board where new words can be displayed. Words need to be read and used more than once before they are stored in permanent memory. Digital cameras let us take instant pictures while children make faces or assume body positions to illustrate words. They may need to take pictures in groups of two or three people to get more precise meanings. Pair each picture with the word it depicts to create an attractive display. Write a poem about the word. Then use a computer to make a card with the picture on the front and the poem inside.

Most of us don't have an extensive vocabulary to draw from, so every household needs a well-worn thesaurus. It is the lumberyard of writing. When we build a house we need building materials. Words are the building blocks of writing, and a thesaurus is where we find appropriate words.

Having said all of this, don't let vocabulary become too much of a concern when engaging in personal writing. The important thing is to get started, and to write in whatever way is comfortable.

OVERCOMING DISABILITIES

BRAD HAS DOWN SYNDROME. When he was quite young Ethel, his mother, was impressed with his ideas, so she began to write them down. Together they composed wonderfully expressive stories and poems.

As they read his intelligent reflections on the events in his life, people began to see Brad in a new way. They would never have realized how insightful he was if Ethel had not started to talk to him about his thoughts, and to put them into written form.

One of Brad's coaches, Val, had a special influence in his life. She moved away and then died suddenly. Here are a few lines from his fairly extensive reflections about her:

> I do have fun with Val every time I see her
> I didn't have a chance to say it back to her
>
> I remember a lot of good things
> Val said, "Brad, you look sharp!"
> I said it back to her!
>
> I remember I bought flowers for her,
> I was so generous!
> She fell in love with me!
> She said, "Brad, you're special!"

Brad became a reader. He started by reading the stories and poems he had created, and soon he was reading other material. Everyone began to see him as capable so he was able to see himself as capable, too. Today he is a wonderful interpretive dancer who performed at the opening of the Special Olympics World Winter Games in Toronto and who continues to charm audiences around the world.

Adults can become scribes for children who have disabilities. Writing draws child and adult together like nothing else. Reading his or her own writing is the best way to teach any special needs person to read. When working with students, I take dictation from all ages and abilities. This allows them freedom to concentrate on ideas while I type. I do my teaching during the editing process.

Families that write unite.

Summary of **K**ey **POINTS**

WRITING *can strengthen family relationships.*
• *Writing requires* **TIME** *and conscious attention.* •
Block off writing time on your calendar. • *Writing
must be* **VALUED** *by parents.* • *By modeling the
art of writing you* **STIMULATE** *your child's desire
to write.* • *Writing can become a* **PLEASURABLE**
habit. • *Help children overcome disabilities by
using writing to* **COMMUNICATE**.

Writing

ACTIVITIES

*"The author of some distinguished
books wrote that I was an inspiration.
All I did was to accept from him a daily
outpouring of his writings."*

—HUGHES MEARNS

Create opportunities to write for an audience.

How do we get our children to become as interested in writing as the author of those distinguished books was during his boyhood? This chapter looks at some practical, easy-to-implement ways to get started writing.

A simple way to initiate family writing is to choose a word, phrase or emotion that everyone can write about. For instance, 'invisible' or 'then he jumped' can inspire even the most reluctant writer to compose two or three sentences. Children are familiar with jumping and most can name things that are invisible.

Practice getting ideas in an order that flows and makes sense by creating a story from everyone's sentences. Have scissors and paper handy. Each person cuts sentences apart and contributes them to the story where they seem to fit. Afterwards, you can re-arrange the parts of the story or add new words and sentences. Paste them on the paper in order. Voila, instant story!

SHARING GOOD LITERATURE

Sharing a common experience through the discussion of an engaging story is the best family-bonding glue available. It presents unique opportunities to discuss all sorts of subjects that would not normally be part of family conversation. For instance, issues to do with appropriate behavior can be discussed by dealing with the way characters in the story behave.

Read a novel or short story aloud, even to older children. Reading can be done around the table, in the car, before bedtime, whenever it can be squeezed in. One of my friends uses CDs that the family listens to when they travel in the car.

Extend the reading to writing. Stop reading at appropriate spots to compose a group response, or to let everyone write their own short summary, or to predict what might happen next. Later, compare the predictions with the way the author chose to develop the story. You might write a letter of advice to a character who is in difficulty. Reflections, reactions and retellings can be presented as prose, poems or songs. We listen to an author more attentively when we accompany reading with writing.

Young writers need experience with as much good literature as possible to learn the best use of words and to discover how stories go together. Reading the work of others is an important source of modeling. One example of how to use a novel as a model for writing is to choose a paragraph that creates a picture of a setting, or one that describes a character. Rewrite it, replacing the adjectives with blanks. Give a copy to each family member with instructions to fill in the adjectives, possibly using the thesaurus as a source.

Reading the new paragraphs aloud makes everyone realize what a difference the choice of adjective makes. In the same way replacing all the 'said' words with 'exclaimed,' 'moaned,' 'babbled,' and so on will totally change the tone of a conversation.

Read passages or headlines from newspapers and magazines aloud. Write stories before or after reading the article. These activities are powerful training for effective writing.

SPECIAL OCCASIONS

Ethan's great-aunt Gail was invited to a baptismal celebration. Each invitation was accompanied by a request from Ethan's parents for a letter to put into a time capsule that he will open on his sixteenth birthday. Here is an excerpt from Gail's letter:

> Your parents, Kim and Sam, have looked forward to your birth all of their lives. Get your mother to pull out the picture of her as a little girl holding her two new baby sisters. Her smile was so big! She loved children. And being part of a loving family was always important to your dad. He truly got a chance when he fell in love with your mom. Together your parents have grown in love for each other as they celebrate family life and love.

A marriage or other special event in the family is a chance to celebrate writing. Ask guests to send stories ahead of time that can be shared during the party. This gives time for the master of ceremonies to find ways to use the stories as part of the program. The stories will not only be entertaining but will make a wonderful memory album.

I attended a funeral recently where many interesting stories were recounted by friends of the deceased, a man who had died tragically in a car accident. The stories were often humorous and they spanned his entire lifetime. If all those stories, and others from friends who didn't have the opportunity to speak, could have been written down and presented to the family, an incredible overview of his life would have been documented.

Stories told by others come from a different perspective and from periods in the life of the deceased that the family often hasn't known about. These stories would create a treasured family heirloom to be passed on to future generations.

When my first grandchild was born I kept a journal in the kitchen by the telephone to record all the interesting little incidents my daughter shared with me. I have a delightful record of stories that would have been totally forgotten. I will put them together in a scrapbook and give it to him on his twelfth birthday. This is so easy to do if you make even sketchy notes right away.

DR. JANE BASKWILL, a professor at Mount St. Vincent University, told me about a tradition that inspires her family to write. Every year her husband and children write a mystery play around her Christmas present. They become characters in the story and produce a video. Jane has to use the video to decipher the clues that enable her to find the present and to guess what it is.

GIFTS CAN ENCOURAGE WRITING

We can celebrate writing through the gifts we give. Cathy Whitman's friend gave her a unique journal. Throughout the book her friend had written questions and favorite quotes at the top of many of the pages. What a great way to personalize a gift for family members and friends! It makes it easier for them to get started writing. Be creative. Think of gifts to give that will encourage others to write.

One woman told me about a routine in her home when she was a child. On Sunday evening everyone sat around the table and wrote a letter to someone. She said she looked forward to these times when they wrote together. They could write to anyone, even to each other.

We can encourage children to write letters to include with gifts. Thank you notes are almost forgotten these days, but they are much appreciated by the recipients. Get your children in the habit of writing to acknowledge gifts, to cheer up sick friends, or to express appreciation to someone who has done them a kindness. A great chance to celebrate writing!

WRITING CAN BE FUN

I had a fun-filled afternoon with my grandson Sean when he was ten years old. I took him to a restaurant filled with sports and music artifacts. Posters of movies and entertainment stars filled the walls to overflowing. Neon lights illuminated exotic bears and even the large washroom sign was red neon.

We entered the restaurant armed with index cards and pens. After ordering, we both began to write descriptions of artifacts and people. We started a new card for each description. Sean moved about the restaurant, quietly identifying and counting the old musical instruments on display. He went on to write about a life-size merry-go-round horse and an old-fashioned light standard. Then both he and I identified all the sports represented by the memorabilia.

On his first card, Sean found that he had to stroke things out and change them. He is fussy about neat work and wanted to rewrite it. I told him we didn't have time and that it didn't matter how messy it was. His writing soul starting to fly, he marked up the second card with abandon! On the way home he made two comments that warmed my heart.

"Now I can finish that story I was trying to write. I have some new ideas," he said, adding, "Grandma, do you have any more of these cards so when we go out to eat I can write while I wait on my food?"

Hurray!

Then I took eight-year-old Bryce. His handwriting is labored so he dictated his descriptions and I wrote for him. When I took five-year-old Rachel and her friend Dianne, they drew pictures while I scribed for them.

What did this experience do for my grandchildren? It helped them to look at things in detail and showed them that writing is detective work and can be fun. It strengthened their emerging sense of self as writers. And it fostered new relationships with Grandma. Now I want to take them to art galleries, the mountains, and shopping malls — anywhere that encourages and inspires us to write together.

WRITE FROM EXPERIENCE

Knowing a lot about a topic makes it easier and more enjoyable to write about it. It is impossible to create without raw material, so we can't write about anything that is not first a part of our experience. When we have a deep understanding of a situation or concept, we can frame appropriate questions that lead to writing. What if? What next? Why not? These are just some of the questions that can only be answered when we are familiar with the subject, or we know where to find the necessary information.

Encourage children to tell what topics they are studying in social studies and science so that everyone can contribute their knowledge to a discussion or can clip articles or watch for books on the topic to help build background. I'm well aware that finding time is the problem with extended discussions in the family. It may mean fewer videos or games or social events but it is vitally important if we are to write intelligently.

TIME-SAVING SUGGESTIONS

While I prefer journals, others may not feel comfortable with such a formal kind of writing — at least not in the beginning. And busy families going in all directions may never get around to writing in them.

A white board with pens and magnets mounted near the kitchen can serve to get writing started. Write messages and encouragements to each other, congratulations for jobs well done, quotes from books being read, poetry, memos, schedules, announcements or anything else that involves writing.

Pieces of writing that are ready for polishing can be attached with a magnet for someone else to edit. Finished writing that is ready for celebration will be very welcome. In a nearby cupboard, store the following supplies so they are readily available for everyone to use — the hard part is getting started.

SUPPLY LIST:

- a variety of thank you notes, special occasion cards and blank cards with interesting pictures on the front

- file cards in a couple of sizes

- pens, pencils, erasers and felt markers

- blank sheets of paper

- sticky notes in various sizes

- a dictionary and a thesaurus

- guides to punctuation and usage

- family address book

EDITING IS IMPORTANT

So far I have focused on generating ideas and producing free-flowing writing, and on encouraging everyone to get in the habit of personal writing. The emphasis has been on just writing and enjoying it. But when we are confident that we have good ideas to share, it is time to learn how to present them well. I have tried to be clear that worthwhile content presented in mechanically correct writing is always the goal.

Never say grammar, spelling and punctuation don't matter. In the early stages, just say that those things don't matter right now — we will deal with them when we have assembled our thoughts.

Polishing writing for others to read is a great confidence builder. We are always pleased when our ideas flow well and elicit positive comments from our readers.

Many parents tell me that they would like to help their children write but they don't know how to do it without writing for them. What follows are some simple editing techniques. They serve two purposes; to help you edit your own writing, and to give you ideas about what to look for when others ask you to help them with their writing.

The best way to begin the editing process is to have the author read the work out loud. It's amazing the discoveries that surface when we perform this simple editing technique. Teachers do this, but it is hard for them to find enough time to listen to all the writing. This is where parents can be of assistance. Students can bring rough drafts of writing home for parents to hear. As they read their piece to you, jot down two or three questions that have to do with the content of the writing, and one or two positive comments. Just don't do the re-writing for them!

Have them put check marks beside the parts that need to be clarified or moved around. It's a good idea to give them time to make changes before editing any further. If the piece is on the computer, this will be easy to do. If it is handwritten, they can cut it apart and paste it back together on another sheet. Next, read through the piece together several times. Here are some suggestions to guide the editing process. Look for the answer to each of these questions in turn. All of these questions will not apply to every piece of writing.

BASIC EDITING QUESTIONS:

- Do most of the sentences start with boring words?
- Have you used bland words such as 'nice' or 'very' instead of more descriptive ones?
- What is the most interesting part? Could it be used as a beginning?
- If it is a story, will the reader be satisfied with the ending?

ADVANCED EDITING QUESTIONS:

- Does the writing reflect the enthusiasm or passion of the writer? Even reports can be energetic and engaging.
- Are the incidents believable? Only books that are based in magic can disregard this rule.
- Does it paint a picture? A basic rule of writing is, "Show, not tell." Even non-fiction can be written so it has a visual sense to it.

- Are the characters well developed? Is there enough information to visualize the person?

- Is there a sense of the place where the action is happening?

- Is the story line clear?

- Does it have an engaging beginning? Well-crafted writing keeps the reader asking, "What next?"

- Does the story have some conflict or problem? Good stories have an element of suspense — problems to be solved, or solutions that may be concealed from the reader until the end.

- Is the closing satisfactory? If it is a story, does it tie up the loose ends?

- Is it too long? Tighten, tighten, tighten! Get rid of unnecessary words!

- Do sentences start with different parts of speech?

WAYS TO START A SENTENCE:

Article/noun	The dog barked loudly as he chased the fleeing tabby cat.
Verb	Barking loudly, the dog...
Verb	Chasing the fleeing tabby cat, the dog...
Preposition	As he chased the fleeing...
Adverb	Loudly barking, the dog chased...
Article/adjective	The tabby cat fled as she was chased...

Here are a couple of tips to make editing easier. Get in the habit of double spacing rough drafts so corrections can be made on the empty line. Use colored pencil for corrections so they are easily spotted. Make students responsible for finding errors. For instance, a simple way to give help that develops spelling consciousness is to say something like, "You have six spelling mistakes. Can you underline them?" When spelling has been corrected add the words to a personal spelling list that can be reviewed on a regular basis. Use questions to draw attention to other kinds of errors as well. "I see something in line three you could correct. What is it?"

Emphasize content first, then provide editing help. Don't spend time on everything that is written. Pick only the best work for polishing. This is the time to seek out a thesaurus, a dictionary and a guide on grammar, sentence structure and punctuation. It's amazing how quickly we can learn the mechanics of writing when we are interested and have a purpose. Maybe you can exchange pieces for editing with another writing family. If you are considering publishing, you will want someone else to have a look at it. Most published writers submit their work to an editor. It's hard to be objective about one's own work.

Use common sense, don't edit every piece for everything. Keep it light. Writing is difficult and learned over time. The goal of family writing is to instill a love of writing and to create successful experiences.

COMPUTERS MAKE IT EASIER

Computers let us move things around, adding or deleting at will. They even inform us about basic spelling and grammar. This saves time and makes editing faster. However, the decisions about changes have to be made by a human so we need to understand how to make our writing better. When writing has been dated and stored in the computer, we can look at how our writing has changed over time. Graphic programs are available that let us quickly create attractive books. Take advantage of them to publish family anthologies that will be treasured for generations. Relatives and friends will be pleased to receive them.

Jean told me she has collected in-jokes along with stories of memorable times and events because of their special significance to her family. These are the kind of stories that say, "You had to be there!"

Family writing is about rewarding and celebrating writing.

Summary of **K**ey **POINTS**

WRITING is an opportunity for family bonding.

• Writing forms close **CONNECTIONS** to reading. •

Celebrations are even more **SPECIAL** with writing.

• A formal record of your special **OCCASION** is

created. • Writing is a great way to have **FUN** with

grandchildren. • **CREATIVITY** is fed by writing.

• Unique **GIFTS** can inspire writing. • Writing

benefits from good editing. • Ask **QUESTIONS,**

don't do it for them.

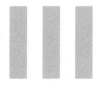

Home and
School

WE ALL NEED TO CELEBRATE WRITING more widely. When schools help parents become more informed writing coaches, those parents become better writers themselves and they, in turn, are better equipped to inspire their children. There are many ways that schools can help parents engage in more family writing. Many of the activities presented in this section come from my own teaching experience; others come from ideas I have picked up over the years. All are intended to spark schools to engage in more writing activities that encourage parents to write with their children.

Writing
PARTNERSHIPS

*"Writing is a gateway to students'
emerging role in our nation's
future as participants and decision
makers in a democratic society."*

—NATIONAL WRITING PROJECT

Powerful things happen when families and schools work together.

Children learn habits, attitudes and values in the home, while the formal teaching of writing is the role of the school. However, our society is becoming increasingly aware that effective education depends on involvement both in the home and at school. What follows are suggestions that can help strengthen the writing partnership between home and school.

Teaching writing is difficult and time consuming. To write well requires that we actually spend time writing. Teachers and parents share many of the same questions. "How can we get students to commit the time and effort needed to become effective writers? How do we overcome resistance to writing? What about students who don't read well, or who can't sit still?"

We become involved with the things we enjoy. When we structure writing so everyone can experience success, it becomes more enjoyable, self-motivating and easier to spend time on.

FORMING PARTNERSHIPS

Schools that form partnerships with parents to celebrate writing as a life skill, with a goal of helping students become competent writers, are off to a good start. Early in the school year, parents and teachers can work together to organize an evening where families come together for what might be called a 'Write-In.' Begin the evening with a short presentation introducing the concept of family writing and the ways in which the school will provide support for those who wish to give it a try.

Show a short video that serves as a story starter, or use some other device to stimulate a theme for the evening. It might be an excerpt from a movie or a passage from a novel. Students might produce a video or perform a play to introduce a topic for writing. Encourage creativity by talking about how writing can be done in different genres such as poetry, songs or monologues.

Each family writes together as a group to finish the story or extend the topic and chooses one member to be the recorder. When they are finished, those who wish to read their compositions aloud can do so. If there's a large crowd, share in small groups. Some families might be willing to bring a favorite dessert or other food item to share, making the evening a true party. What an incredible boost this event will be to the celebration of writing. Plan another evening in January to start the new year. People are creative when they brainstorm. Teachers and parents will find many ways to make 'Write-Ins' highlights of the school year. For instance, it could be a theme night with participants in costume if they wish. That would add to the fun!

Teachers can also invite parents to attend writing lessons in their classrooms where parents can learn about writing and spend time composing with their children. Two or three classes could cooperate in raising money to bring in a professional writer to do a workshop. Participating in writing together at school is a great way to help parents improve their own writing while strengthening teacher-child-parent partnerships.

We learn best by reflecting on what we have heard, and by organizing our knowledge to fit with prior experience. Even young children can write using strong words and big ideas if someone puts the building blocks into their experience. Teachers and parents have an important task — the building of knowledge and curiosity about words, and about the world. Many teachers these days do a great job of getting students to write in journals. They make writing part of all subjects, including math. Quiet time set aside for writing is never wasted time! Days must not become so busy, nor curriculum demands so heavy, that we omit this vital step to learning. It is in silence that we can hear ourselves think. Community writing, at home and at school, is powerful.

INSTRUCTIVE FEEDBACK

Instructive feedback is identifying the habits and attitudes you want to encourage, and then commenting when people are engaged in them. Look for something to praise, no matter how small, in each student's writing every month. Don't tell them you are doing it, just do it casually while they are writing or sharing. Comment on specific attributes that will benefit the writing of the whole class. "Jody, I love the adjectives you used to describe that clown. I can see him in my mind."

Keep a checklist to ensure that every student receives praise. A brief note home to the child's parents, repeating the compliment, teaches parents what to look for in effective writing and enables them to discuss writing in a more informed way. And, of course, parents are delighted to get good news. Praise is a huge confidence builder and reinforces the qualities we value. Praise takes little time, instills confidence, and transforms attitudes toward writing. Julia Cameron observes that, "As a writing teacher, it is my experience that if I praise a student's strengths, the weaknesses eventually fall away." I find the same thing to be true in my work with children and their parents.

Readers are an intimate part of the circle of writing. Readers who appreciate, benefit from, or reject our work serve an important purpose in affirming us as writers. By giving lots of instructive feedback — the type of feedback that identifies the skills needed to become more effective writers — writing becomes stronger and more rewarding.

LISTENING IS A KEY

The best way to demonstrate esteem and respect for children is to listen, with your total attention, while they read their work. They learn to value themselves and their writing and to see themselves as competent. It allows for feedback that is specific and thus more valuable. Parents and teachers who do focused listening serve as models so students learn to become better listeners. The need for focused listening is never outgrown and I am most grateful when someone takes time to listen to me or to read my work and give me honest feedback.

NATALIE GOLDBERG, in *Writing Down the Bones,* says that writing is ninety percent listening. By listening with all our senses we capture reality and it pours out in our writing. She gives good advice on how to become a good writer, "Read a lot, listen well and deeply, and write a lot. And don't think too much. Just enter the heat of words and sounds and colored sensations and keep your pen moving across the page."

LOCATION, LOCATION, LOCATION

The habit of writing wherever we happen to be is a good one. Describing our location makes us more observant in our everyday lives. Holidays are perfect for this. It is impossible for whole classes to go to a variety of locations to write, but students can make journal entries describing the places they visit. They can use pictures taken on vacation to write descriptions later. Cafés, bedrooms, skateboard parks, fashion shows and shopping malls also provide excellent backgrounds for stories. The list is endless. This is an excerpt from twelve-year-old Gordon's entry while visiting Kelowna, British Columbia.

At our grandparents our first thing we did was hug! After an introduction to their renovated backyard they explained that the roaring mountain park fire was the biggest fire across

Canada. The Okanagan Mountain Park fire was on the move and had already taken some houses situated along the cliffs of the Okanagan Lake. The fire couldn't be reached by fire-fighters because of the rugged terrain forcing water bombers to fight a losing battle. On our seventh day we were put on evacuation alert and eventually evacuated. We left our grand-parent's home wistfully and stayed at a hotel on the opposite side of Kelowna. Soon it was time for us to leave. Against our will, we headed back to Calgary.

COLLECTING BIOGRAPHIES

My favorite things include listening to someone who has read or traveled extensively, who has worked in an industry about which I have little understanding, or who has lived in a country that is not familiar to me. How many biographies from all walks of life are available to young readers? Probably not a lot. Such writing can inform students of the different career choices and lifestyles available to them in our wonderfully varied world. Unaware of the possibilities, many simply choose the familiar vocation of their mother or father. Stories from mechanics, engineers, truck drivers, air traffic controllers, artists, ski patrollers, surveyors and so on are interesting reading material for young readers. What a rich addition it would be to the school library if parents and other community members contributed stories about their work, and students used their skills to edit the stories and publish them as books for the school library. Another celebration of family writing!

TRAVELING STORIES

Writing can be initiated by choosing the opening paragraph of a story or novel as a story starter. Folk tales work especially well. Someone writes the next episode and passes it to another class member.

It circulates until everyone has added an episode to one of the story starters. Circulate each story starter about five times. The fifth person has to bring the story to a conclusion. The beginning of the tale of *Tom Thumb*, taken from Grimm's Fairy Tales, is an example of a story starter.

> There was once a tailor who had a son no higher than a thumb, so he was called Tom Thumb. Notwithstanding his small size, he had plenty of spirit. One day he said to his father, "Father, go out into the world I must and will."
> "Very well, my son," said the old man. And taking a long darning needle, he put a knob of sealing-wax on the end saying, "Here is a sword to take with you on your journey and here is a little bag that has food and drink inside it."

Every story will take Tom through a totally different adventure. Sharing the completed stories will present opportunities for mini-lessons. Appoint a group of students to integrate as many of the episodes as possible. Present them in a 'soap opera' format by reading a piece each day on the intercom or by choosing students to read an episode each day to a younger class.

Stories can also go back and forth between classrooms. I did this with teachers in five different schools. Each teacher sent a story starter to the next school on the list. Every student in that class wrote a next episode. Students voted on the one that would be added before it was sent on to the next school. The fifth school concluded the story and it was circulated again for the classes to read. In the end, five great stories were generated and writing was celebrated.

Cooperative writing is a way to connect families and schools. The teacher sends home a story starter for a family to add an episode. When it is returned it is sent to another family and so on until about four families have a chance to add to the plot. The fifth family is asked to bring it all together with a suitable ending. Families can choose to put their names on their contribution if they wish. A copy of the completed story is sent to each participating family. It is great fun and another way to celebrate writing together.

TAKING A POINT OF VIEW

Here are some examples that will help you take a different approach to writing and expand your imagination.

1. Write about an event in the story as a journalist reporting the incident.

2. Make scripts for movies from your favorite scenes and produce them.

3. Choose a quote that is debatable and share your reflections.

4. Become a character and write a monologue as that person, animal, or inanimate object.

5. Change a newspaper article into poetry.

USING READING NOTEBOOKS

Teachers can help families explore books together by teaching students how to reflect as they read. Read a short story or book aloud. At appropriate intervals, stop reading and have everyone write a sentence or two of reflection, define a new word from context, or form a question. Keep entries short. The goal is to make the habit of using journals to comment on what is being read so comfortable that it becomes a life-long activity. Lev Vygotsky, a well-known Russian psychologist who pioneered research in developmental psychology, observed, "What they can do with help today, they can do by themselves tomorrow."

Here is an example of nine-year-old Scott's journal entry written while reading *Matilda* by Roald Dahl. He found this episode especially funny and revealing of Matilda's character.

> Another example of how Matilda causes trouble. She is really mad at her Dad. In the morning when she wakes up she puts her Mom's Platinum blond hair dye into Dad's hair gel. Matilda is in the dining room eating her cornflakes and waiting for her Dad to appear she suddenly hears her Dad's voice booming down the hall. He comes into the dining room then his wife comes in and yells what have you done to your hair. A huge commotion started. Get me a mirror he orders and sees his black hair has turned white. Get me an emergency appointment with your hairdresser!

Well-crafted books, short stories and novels have universal qualities to which everyone can relate. When I read *The Snow Goose* by Paul Gallico to a grade six class, I remember the reaction of one boy in particular. Jason was quiet and participated only when necessary. He resisted writing. But when he was able to write from the viewpoint of Rhayder, the rejected hero, he wrote with remarkable clarity. It was safe to express his ideas through Rhayder. I was better able to serve as his teacher when I realized that Jason was able to share his important ideas through story characters.

When writing is rewarded both at home and at school it becomes an activity pursued not just for grades, but for the satisfaction it gives to the writer.

Cooperation builds strong bridges.

Summary of Key POINTS

Writing well is important. • **SUCCESS** *in school is affected by writing skills.* • *Writing can be strengthened by teacher-parent* **PARTNERSHIPS**. • *Parents can act as editors for their children's writing.* • *Encouragement helps* **BUILD** *good writers.* • *Start a lifelong* **HABIT** *of making writing a part of life.* • *Writing thoughts in a journal has many* **BENEFITS**. • *Celebrate writing and watch it blossom.*

Writing at
SCHOOL

*"Writing is the most visible
expression not only of what students
know but of how they have
learned it."*

—NATIONAL WRITING PROJECT

Schools are where children learn to write.

▬ Teachers of writing must write. One way to model writing is to create occasions when teachers write in their own journals while the students are writing. "I'm sorry. You will have to do the best you can. I'm busy writing now," is an attitude that sets the stage for students to write freely during the composition stage and contributes to the class becoming a community of writers.

All teachers are responsible for developing good writing in their subject areas. They build listening and writing skills by taking time in class to write after new material has been presented. Students write the new ideas in their own words. This can be varied by having them write in pairs so they can engage in dialogue to refine understanding. No one judges the quality of the writing. Free-writing is a check on how well concepts are understood. If a few students share what they have written, it serves as a review of what has been taught and as an opportunity for further clarification by the teacher. It is also informative to have students write what they know about a new topic before it is taught.

FOR BETTER UNDERSTANDING

If I had the privilege of being in an elementary classroom again I would write a short story about each student, projecting him or her into the future and creating a successful life for each, based on perceived strengths. I might start with a child who has a special problem, for whatever reason, or maybe a shy child who resists attempts to be drawn into the flow of life in the classroom, or a student who doesn't have many friends. Eventually I would try to write about them all.

The process would force me to look for positives in even the most difficult students. It would give me new insights into ways to deal with diverse personalities and situations. I might find ways to help them fit more easily and successfully into life. Students would be able to see themselves in a different way if I gave them their stories. In the same way, parents can write positive stories about their children. It creates strong bonds.

CLARIFYING IDEAS FOR PRESENTATION

RICK IS A TEACHER who worked for many years as a counselor. When he discovered I was writing about writing, he wanted me to pass on a tip that he gave to all the young people he worked with. When preparing for formal conversations, organize your presentation in writing, says Rick. A job interview is always difficult, but it will be much easier if you write about the strengths you have to bring to the position, your expectations and the questions you need to ask. A trip to see your doctor or any other professional will be more successful if you write questions and pertinent information beforehand.

Confronting someone about a situation that needs to be addressed will go more smoothly if you take time to analyze the problem and the way in which you are going to approach it in writing. Thinking about solutions and writing them down helps achieve clarity.

EVALUATION AS A TEACHING TOOL

Evaluating writing is difficult and time-consuming for the teacher, and papers that have every error marked can be discouraging for the writer. One way to solve this dilemma is for teachers to inform the students what the focus for a particular assignment will be. Each writing assignment doesn't have to be graded in everything that can go wrong. With one or two areas of concentration, the assignment becomes an achievable, rather than an overwhelming, task. Sending the project home with an explanation identifying the specific skill being practiced is an effective way to educate parents on the writing process.

USSW

DAVID BOUCHARD, a Canadian author, educator and presenter says, in *The Gift of Reading,* "I believe no school should be without a school-based, silent-reading program." David visits many schools and he observed that those who didn't have a structured silent-reading program took away from the impression that reading was a valued activity in the school. Reading lacked official endorsement.

I think we could — and should — substitute the word writing for reading in David's observations and begin to give it the same status. Many schools have USSR — Uninterrupted Sustained Silent Reading — a time when everyone in the school drops what they are doing and reads for twenty minutes. How about doing the same for writing every third or fourth day? Simply substitute writing for reading.

Students need a separate USSW journal so that they can write ongoing episodes from session to session. An easy way to support family writing is for students to take these journals home for further writing and sharing.

ORAL LANGUAGE AND WRITING

A major difficulty with writing arises when students have to frame an argument, analyze the propositions of another, or synthesize varying points of view. Learning to organize an argument orally is the first step toward being able to write critically.

The ability to effectively state opinions on relevant topics is so important in the maturation process. Speaking in front of an audience is the number one fear of most people, and the prospect of a job interview is also high on the fear-factor list. They are really the same. In both cases we risk embarrassing ourselves before others. When we are interviewed for a job we are asked to tell our story. The more competently we can do this, the more chance we have of getting the job. The ability to tell a joke, to relay a personal story and to converse easily in public are valuable assets in personal and professional situations.

Every home and classroom needs a video camera so students can see and hear themselves reading their stories, engaging in discussions, producing documentaries, creating advertisements and so on. As they review the footage with another student or a family member, they will discover ways to improve their speaking ability. Re-filming the work until the participants are satisfied can be a huge learning experience and another way to celebrate writing.

Writing would be improved if we could offer courses in public speaking as part of the education process. This probably won't happen soon. The challenge is for teachers to find ways to provide more speaking opportunities, and for parents to coach children in presenting their ideas more clearly.

WRITING SUCCESS FOR EVERYONE

In my experience, boys resist writing more than girls. Maybe they don't see many men in their lives writing and view it as a girl thing. One of the most valuable results of family writing is for boys to see their fathers involved in personal writing.

In the right environment, boys become incredibly interested and capable writers. I'll always remember Luigi, a reluctant writer in grade six. We were writing poetry around the theme of color. Luigi wrote a short, graphic poem about how he felt when he thought of the color blue. Everyone loved his poem. When it was time to write in his journal, Luigi came to my desk and quietly asked if I would mind if he wrote poetry in his journal. Would I mind!

Blue as the sky and
The high, white puffy
Marshmallows floating on top
And the big fire-ball shooting
Light, all over the blue waters.
Blue is gentle.

Writing poetry is one of the best ways students can learn new words and how to use them powerfully. Steven was another of my boys who did not see himself as a capable writer. At the end of our study of Monsters and Heroes, each student chose a monster prevalent in our society. They wrote about drugs, war, poverty, pollution. Steven wrote a poem about unemployment that helped him to begin to enjoy writing.

When you work you have
Lots of money, food and pleasure.
But a monster creeps around the world
Taking jobs away
You could end up with nothing

Younger boys like to use plots, characters and locations from television shows, cartoons, movies and computer games. Stories where they combine characters from visual mediums with ones from books are creative. Mixing up characters such as Frodo, Mario, Shrek, Spiderman, Harry Potter and Bilbo Baggins stimulates imaginative writing.

A REASON FOR WRITING

ANNE-MARIE WIGLE, a teacher in Dartmouth, Nova Scotia, told me about a project that her class of eight students with learning difficulties did with three grade five classes in her school. It would be a good activity for families to do at home too. Students chose someone who was an important influence in their lives. They wrote stories and poems to express their feelings about this special person. They packaged their writing, along with pictures, poetry and other appropriate artifacts, and presented it as a Christmas gift.

The process of writing and compiling the material for the gift was exciting for the students, but the surprise and joy expressed by the recipients made it a truly wonderful experience. While the students were working on their projects, Anne-Marie created a portfolio of appreciation for her brother, who had been especially influential in shaping her life. Her whole family cried when he read the pieces aloud around the Christmas tree.

Writing for a real audience is stimulating.

Summary of Key POINTS

WRITING is time-consuming to teach and grade.

• Teachers **BENEFIT** when parents are editors. • Writers suffer when insensitively judged. • If labeled inadequate too early, **POTENTIAL** can wither away. • Boys may need special encouragement. • Everyday activities can be used to **STIMULATE** imagination. • Success sparks the desire to write. • Speech **TRAINING** enhances writing.

*"Finally, one has to just shut up,
sit down and write."*

—Natalie Goldberg

We all have a basic need to feel important and to be celebrated.

Jerome Bruner says that "We get interested in what we get good at." We have to see the possibility of success before we can actually experience it. This means celebrating each small step of progress.

I can't think of a better example than infants learning to speak. Their first attempts are far from accurate, but we celebrate them as joyous occasions. Our little darling says, "Gug, gug," and we phone Grandma to tell her that the baby just said, "Milk." We model and repeat words for them without judgment, and for as long as it takes to get it right. We treat them as speakers.

One mother told me that her two-year-old son said, "Doo datta doo wah," for "I want a drink of water." Did they take him for speech lessons? Of course not! The family celebrated by asking for water in the same way. They had confidence that he would grow up speaking well so they just enjoyed the process.

We should assume the same relaxed sense of acceptance and enjoyment as our children grow into successful writers. The love of writing can be instilled at an early age by capturing children's stories on paper and then re-reading the stories to them. No matter how much like a desert a child seems, somewhere within is a spring of water that makes him or her special. Writing helps us to tap into that well, to uncover the hidden gifts. Writing enables us to examine the invisible, giving it concrete form and making it more tangible. Later, when we revisit our written record of the emotions and circumstances surrounding an event, we are better equipped to understand the invisible forces that were present. The insights gained through writing help us to devise solutions and to make plans for similar circumstances in the future.

Writing is practical and democratic. Anyone can write. No special equipment is required. We all have raw material to work with — it's called life experience. Situations and relationships are constantly changing, so we have continuous fuel for our writing fire.

Who decides what degree of quality one needs to be a writer? We can all enjoy cooking even though we aren't chefs. We just do it.

Families need the support of schools if they are to become success-ful at implementing family writing. Parents and teachers working together can cooperate to find new ways to celebrate the written word and to give writing more status in society.

Things that evoke strong emotions leave vivid memories. People tell me that they don't write because they got the message, by the way their writing was graded and labeled, that they couldn't write well. It is critical not to destroy the bud with excessive judgment before it has a chance to flower. Emphasizing strengths at home and at school builds positive experiences that enable everyone to experience the joy of writing. Children who have already experienced success at home will find it easier to develop into competent writers at school.

In *Free Play*, Stephen Nachmanovitch says, "The easiest way to do art is to do away with failure altogether and just get on with it." Let's concentrate on commenting and reporting on the successes in each child's writing, do away with failure, and just get on with it.

The sign on the bus stop says, "Read With Your Children." We have National Reading Week every year. The International Reading Association promotes reading and advocates that parents read with their children. Early literacy programs supply books to families and counsel them on the importance of modeling reading.

Our society does not celebrate writing in the same way. We celebrate our successful writers but we have few organized celebrations that promote writing for everyone. This book argues that when families celebrate writing, children will be more likely to enjoy it, and they will write more effectively. Families benefit by having better personal histories on record, and everyone benefits from the presence of stronger ideas presented by more articulate writers.

If I could leave you with only one message from this book, it would stress the importance of personal and collective writing. Developing the habit of personal writing will help you shape your innermost thoughts, articulate your opinions in public and deepen your understanding of people and events. When you celebrate writing in the family unit, all of society benefits. Your life, and the future of your children, will take on new promise as you become engaged in the process of writing and of raising effective writers.

We all deserve to be celebrated.

Bibliography RESOURCES

Aftel, Mandy. *The Story Of Your Life — Becoming the Author of Your Experience*. New York: Simon & Schuster, 1996.

Berton, Pierre. *The Joy of Writing*. Anchor Canada: Random House, 2003.

Bouchard, David. *The Gift of Reading*. Victoria: Orca Book Publishers, 2001.

Bruner, Jerome. *The Culture of Education*. Cambridge: Harvard University Press, 1996.

Cameron, Julia. *The Right to Write*. New York: Tarcher Putnam Inc., 1999.

Dahl, Roald. *Matilda*. New York: Scholastic, 1996.

Flagg, Fannie. *Fried Green Tomatoes*. From Conrad, Barnaby. *Snoopy's Guide to the Writing Life*. Cincinnati: Writer's Digest Books, 2002.

Fredricksson, Marianne. *Hanna's Daughters*. London: Orion Books, 1998.

Gallico, Paul. *The Snow Goose*. New York: Alfred Knopf, 1984.

Goldberg, Natalie. *Writing Down the Bones*. Boston: Shambhala Publications, 1986.

Greene, Ross W. *The Explosive Child*. New York: HarperCollins Publishers, 2001.

Hutchins, Pat. *Rosie's Walk*. New York: Simon and Schuster, 1968.

Johnson, Basil. *Ojibway Heritage*. Toronto: McClelland and Stewart, 1984.

Kabat-Zinn, Jon. *Wherever You Go There You Are: Mindfulness Meditation In Everyday Life*. New York: Hyperion, 1994.

Kidder, Tracy. From National Writing Project & Carl Nagin, *Because Writing Matters*. San Francisco: Jossey-Bass, 2003.

Light, Richard J. *Making the Most of College*. Cambridge: Harvard University Press, 2001.

Mearns, Hughes. *Every Child Has a Gift* taken from *Getting the Most out of Life*. Reader's Digest Association, 1955.

Nachmanovitch, Stephen. *Free Play: Improvisation in Life and Art.* New York: Tarcher Putnam, 1990.

National Writing Project & Carol Nagin. *Because Writing Matters.* San Francisco: Jossey-Bass, 2003

Nelson, G. Lynn. *Writing and Being: Taking Back Our Lives Through the Power of Language.* San Diego: LuraMedia Inc., 1994 .

Nichols, John. Taken from Cameron, Julia. *The Artist's Way.* New York: Tarcher Putnam, 1992.

Rawls, Wilson. *Where the Red Fern Grows.* Delacorte Books for Young Readers, 1996.

Ross, Rupert. *Returning To The Teachings: Exploring Aboriginal Justice.* Toronto: Penguin Books, 1996.

Smith, Frank. *Writing and the Writer.* New York: Holt, Rinehart and Winston, 1982.

The Brothers Grimm. *Household Stories.* New York: Dover Publications, 1963.

Zinsser, William. *On Writing Well.* New York: HarperCollins Publishers, 1994.

SUGGESTED REFERENCE BOOKS

Allen, Robert. *Punctuation.* Oxford: Oxford University Press, 2002. You'll use this one lots.

Allen, Robert. *Spelling.* Oxford: Oxford University Press, 2002. You will probably use this one more than you think.

Allen, Roberta. *The Playful Way to Serious Writing.* Boston: Houghton Mifflin, 2002. An inspiring book of writing starters.

Ballenger, Bruce & Lane, Barry. *Discovering the Writer Within.* Cincinnati Writer's Digest Books, 1989. If you're trying to become a writer, this is one of the best books you can buy.

Billingham, Jo. *Editing and Revising Text.* Oxford: Oxford University Press, 2002. More than most people need to know but a valuable reference.

Casey, Fitts & Hawley. *Effective Letters for Every Occasion*. New York: Barron's Educational Series, 2000. Helps to revive the almost-lost practice of personal letter writing.

Conrad, Barnaby & Schulz, Monte. *Snoopy's Guide to the Writing Life*. Cincinnati: Writer's Digest Books 2002. Excellent inspiration for writers at any level of experience.

Heffron, Jack. *The Writer's Idea Workshop: How to make your good ideas great*. Cincinnati: Writer's Digest Books, 2003. Makes turning good ideas into great writing a pleasure.

Lamb, Sandra E. *How To Write It*. Berkeley: Ten Speed Press, 1998. A complete guide to everything you'll ever write.

Lane, Barry. *Writing as a Road to Self-Discovery*. Cincinnati: Writer's Digest Books, 1993. Writing ideas for practice.

Parsons, Les. *Revising and Editing*. Markham: Pembroke, 2001. More tips on revising and editing.

SPELLING

Morris, Thea. *Spelling Rules! Grades 1-3*. Reprinted with permission. Winnipeg: Portage & Main Press, 2000.

Morris, Thea. *Making Spelling Fun! Ideas that Work Grades 1-6* Winnipeg: Portage & Main Press, 1994

Snowball, Diane; Bolton, Faye. *Spelling K-8: Planning and Teaching*. Portland: Stenhouse Publishers, 1999.

SPELLING AND VOCABULARY

BALDERDASH
Phony definitions — increases root word knowledge. Mattel, 12 up.

BOGGLE
Three-minute word game for spelling words. Parker, 8 up.

DICTIONARY DABBLE
A word definition bluffing game. Patch, 10 up.

4-WAY SPELL DOWN
Roll of the dice spelling fun. Parker Bros., 12 up.

JUMBLE
Unscramble words on a surprise-filled gameboard. Cadaco, 8 up.

MAD GAB
Listening skills uncover words. Hilarious fun. Patch, 10 up.

MY WORD!
Word game that plays like a party game. Out of the Box Pub, 12 up.

PASSWORD
Antonyms, synonyms, vocabulary. Endless Games, 8 up.

PERQUACKY
Word building. Cardinal Industries, 3 up.

SCRABBLE
Building crosswords. Milton Bradley, 8 up.

SCRABBLE JR.
Building words. Milton Bradley, younger children.

TABOO
Vocabulary and thesaurus practice. Hasbro, 12 up.

TABOO JR.
200 words picked specially for kids. Hasbro, under 12.

TAKE FOUR WORD GAME.
Word building, problem solving, creativity, strategic thinking.
Learning Resources, 9 up.

TRIBOND
Lateral thinking. What do these items have in common?
Patch, numerous versions.

WHEEL OF FORTUNE
Hangman with big wheel for prizes. Pressman, 8 up.

WORD RUMMY
Using spelling to build words. Cadaco, 7 up.

You will never think the same way about words and how to make sense of language again!

Vera has been given a special gift — the ability to communicate simply and clearly. Her exuberant energy, natural sense of humor and timely stories add the spice necessary to ensure memorable presentations. Vera has spoken to many educators, parents, volunteers, women's groups and conferences on education and motivational topics.

COMMENTS FROM PARTICIPANTS:

- Very hands-on, practical information

- Honesty, open discussion of issues and very informative

- Please have her back — many parents could benefit...

- Excellent speaker. I really learned new ideas

Vera Goodman's wisdom, unique insights and ability to engage the audience guarantees a great learning experience for everyone. Vera is unique and fascinating — she is definitely one of a kind!

Ask Vera to tailor a presentation to your needs today.

Website: www.readingwings.com
E-mail: info@readingwings.com
Toll-Free: **1-800-411-9660**

"Vera informed and entertained our audience consistently."

Margaret Reid – *Principal*

SiMPlY Read!

Helping Others Learn *to* Read

(formerly *Reading is More Than Phonics!*)

"As soon as I finished reading *Simply Read* I knew I wanted to put it in the hands of parents in my school. Thanks for giving us a very useful tool to help parents better understand the complex task of learning how to read."

Karen Wesley, Elementary School Principal

A simple, common sense approach that greatly simplifies the process of learning to read for parents helping beginning readers as well as for those who serve as reading coaches to older students and adults.

These proven techniques have helped thousands of beginning and challenged readers learn quickly and with comprehension. *Simply Read!* is rewarding, enriching and inspiring — parents and teachers confirm this book is an invaluable resource at home and in school.

Vera believes that knowledge of phonics is important but that it can also be the reason children get blocked and discouraged on their way to becoming successful readers. Her company, Reading Wings Inc., is a professional organization that assists parents and teachers in overcoming reading difficulties.

"Our library appreciates your book. It is very clear and your strategies are ones that parents can easily put into practice! When parents need help it is the first book I reach for."

Kathleen S. Linn, Youth Services Librarian

A must-read for parents of pre-schoolers and adolescent non-readers.

AVAILABLE AT BOOKSTORES

For more information: **1-800-411-9660** / www.readingwings.com

About the **AUTHOR**

Vera Goodman's lifelong commitment to help struggling readers find pleasure and meaning in reading led her to create Reading Wings, a unique coaching program focusing on the experiences and enjoyment that coaches and students share as they learn together. Vera has taken her distinctive coaching style and cutting-edge strategies to a wide variety of audiences. Her vivacious personality and sparkling energy have endeared her to thousands of people who have been influenced by her bestselling first book, *Reading is More than Phonics!* (now re-published as *Simply Read*), or by her dynamic presentations and powerful teaching video, *Coaching Young Readers.*

As a teacher, administrator, conference speaker and workshop facilitator for many years, Vera is recognized as a leading authority in teaching children and adults how to become competent and enthusiastic readers. In her latest book, *Simply Write,* she shares inspiring stories, common-sense tips and delightful insights into writing for all ages.

Vera's work was celebrated by Global Television in 2003 when she received the Woman of Vision award for her contributions to literacy. Recently she was honored by Seattle Pacific University, her alma mater, with the Medallion Award for excellence and outstanding service in her field. On graduating from Central Collegiate High School in Moose Jaw, Saskatchewan, she received the Governor General's Medal for scholarship. She has an MA in language arts from the University of Calgary.

Vera has three daughters. She lives in Calgary, Alberta, Canada where she spends as much time as possible with her three grandchildren. One of her hobbies is riding her horse, Missy, in the foothills.